Swing

Expert Advice For Novice Traders

–

How To Minimize Your Losses And Maximize Your Gains Using Actionable Entry And Exit Strategies, Pragmatic Analysis Tools, And Effective Guiding Principles

Andrei D. Carlson

Table Of Contents:

Introduction - The 7 Steps Of Effective Swing Trades

The very first question that you may be going through your mind is, "what is swing trading?" Swing trading refers to an active form of selling in which the trader identifies intermediate opportunities by utilizing a wide range of technical analysis.

The main reason why swing trading uses technical analysis is based on its short-term nature of trades. However, you have to note that fundamental analysis goes a long way in enhancing the overall analysis. For instance, if the swing trader recognizes a bullish setup in stocks, there may need to verify that the asset fundamentals are favorable and are likely to improve.

Think of swing trading as a strategy whose main aim is taking on small gains in the short-term while still ensuring that losses are cut down fast. The benefits may be lower at first, but when you trade consistently over some time, you will accumulate excellent returns annually. You can swing a trade for a few days to weeks, but you could also hold the position for longer.

With swing trading, instead of targeting 20-25% profits on stocks, the profit goals are a little modest and ranges between 5-10%, especially in more robust markets. It is reasonable to think that these profits are not life-changing rewards. However, the one crucial thing you should focus on is the time factor.

Your primary focus as a swing trader is not on gains that you accumulate over weeks or months. This is mainly because the average length of the trade typically lies between 5-10 days. This means that making a big win within this time is not realistic. However, it is the small wins that eventually add up to give you significant returns overall. For instance, if you get 20% gains every month, then a gain of 5-10% each week has the potential to add up to significant profits in the end.

Well, what of the losses? The truth is that you need to factor in the losses you make. If you realize smaller gains, then they will only yield to growing your portfolio if the losses are kept minimal. Instead of maintaining stop loss at 7-8%, you must maintain them at a maximum of 2-3%. This way, you ensure that you maintain a 3:1 profit-to-loss ratio, which is a sound management rule for your portfolio if you are considering success. Otherwise, having an outsized loss risk will wipe away all the progress you make with smaller gains.

That said, one thing that you need to bear in mind is that swing trading will help you deliver more substantial gains on individual trades. Your sticks have the potential of exhibiting a significant strength at the start that you can leverage for bigger gains. You could also take partial profits while ensuring that there is still room for growth.

Swing Trading Vs. Day trading Vs. Trend Trading

Swing trading and day trading are somewhat similar practices, but the primary distinguishing factor between the two is time. One thing that you will notice is that the time frames in which you hold the trades are different. For day traders, you are in and out of the trade within a few minutes to hours. However, in the case of swing trading, you trade over several days to weeks or even longer.

The short time frame held by day traders means that they do not own this position overnight. Because of this, you bridge the gap of news announcements coming in after hours and risking a big move against them. However, for a swing trader, you have to stay wary of stocks opening that are significantly different from how they closed the previous day.

The other important point to note is that there is an added risk when working with shorter time frames. This is mainly because a wide gap between the bid, ask, and commission can eat significantly into your profits. This is something that swing traders struggle with a lot. However, the effect is even more amplified in the case of day traders. This is because they may end up doing all the work, while brokers and market makers enjoy all the benefits.

Day traders often have the opportunity to take advantage of their portfolios with wider margins, at least four times the purchasing power to offset these gaps. When more significant leveraged positions are taken, there is a probability that increased percentage gains will be realized, which offsets the costs. That said, you have to realize that you will not be right all the time; no one is.

In other words, you have to be focused and disciplined to ensure that trades do not go against you in a big way. Otherwise, one bad trade might blow up on your account, causing a loss to your portfolio, and the chances of recovery may be slim. On the other hand, for a swing trader, incurring a string of losses or one significant loss still has dramatic effects. However, the lower leverage lowers the chances of the outcome wiping out your portfolio.

This is something that leads to a time-related difference referred to as time commitment. For you to perform proper day trading, you must focus all your attention on various positions. This is to ensure that you continuously look for new opportunities to replace your current position. Therefore, if you have been thinking of trading as a side job, it is time you consider day trading your only job.

Note that the additional time commitment you take day trading is accompanied with many risks. When you do not have a steady paycheck, your income becomes reliant on day trading, and this adds another layer of stress and emotions, which risks poor decision-making.

However, when swing trading, there are days when you have few transactions and nothing on others. The good thing is that you can check positions periodically or even handle them with the help of alerts. This way, you will know when critical price points have been reached instead of constant monitoring. This way, you can diversify your investment and keep a level head as a swing trader.

What is trend trading?

Trend trading is a style of trading that tries to capture gains by analyzing the momentum of an asset in a specific direction. Now, you might have noticed that the prices often fluctuate in one overall direction at a time. That is, it may be going up or down, and that is referred to as a trend.

When there is are indications that the trend is going in an upward direction, trend traders enter a long position. This is mainly because higher swing lows and swing highs often accompany an uptrend. On the other hand, when an asset trend low, then the trend traders opt to get into a short position mainly because lower swing lows and highs accompany a downtrend.

The most important question however is, how does trend trading work?

When it comes to trend trading strategies, the assumption here is that a security will keep moving in a similar direction as the current trend. It is such strategies that are composed of stop-loss or take-profit provision for it to avoid losses or lock-in profits in case a trend reversal was to occur.

Short-, intermediate-, and long-term traders often prefer using trend trading. For them to identify the direction of the trend and the possible time of shift, price action and other technical tools are used.

One thing to bear in mind is that you need to pay attention to the price movements on a chart when trend trading. In the case of an uptrend, you will see that the prices move above the current highs while they stay above prior swings when prices drop. This is an indicator that although the prices are fluctuating, the overall trajectory is up.

This same concept applies when there are downtrends because the traders are watching out for prices to make overall lower highs and lows. When this is not happening, then this may mean that the downtrend is in question or is complete.
Therefore, the trend trader loses interest in holding a short position.

Now, you may be wondering, whether day, swing or trend trading is more profitable? Well, the truth is that irrespective of what kind of trader you are, profitability will be dependent on your ability to apply a vast array of technical tools in analyzing the market or security.

The bottom line is, swing, day, and trend traders often execute market-timing strategies that need a variety of skills. Although experienced traders can successfully mix and match strategies, new traders need to pay attention to one approach that works well with them and stick with it until they have mastered it fully.

How To Start Trading

Swing trading is a directional trading strategy that you can learn to implement in your market view. With the following steps, you will learn how to use a simple options strategy such as buying a call or put so that you can comfortably swing trade in any financial asset market where options are available to you.

Step 1 Select an asset to trade

When it comes to swing trading, the very first step is to select the underlying asset to the business, once you have identified a trading opportunity. Your role as a swing trader is to ensure that you monitor varied asset markets to increase your chances of finding a good setup for a trade.

When choosing an asset to trade, you must identify one that is due for a correction. You can achieve this by using a momentum indicator like RSI. It is this indicator that serves as a bounded oscillator whose role is to inform whether a market is overbought or undersold. A market that is oversold is one whose value is above 70, while one that is undersold is one whose value is below 30.

The secret is for you to purpose to sell when the RSI value is higher than 70 and purchase when the value is below 30. If you want highly reliable swing trading signals from RSI, you must wait until the occurrence of price-RSI divergence. This means that the price makes a greater extreme in a move like hitting a new high. This is a brilliant swing trade signal you can use to know when the market is due for an imminent correction.

Step 2 Select a direction to go

Now that you have identified a market and used a suitable form of market analysis in determining the trading opportunity with a risk/reward ratio of >2:1, the next step is for you to take a directional market view based on underlying assets. You can do this by using call or put options.

For instance, if you expect that the market is going to rise, then the best scenario for you is the call option, which offers you limited downside risk as well as unlimited upside potential. On the other hand, if you anticipate that the market will fail, then you would purchase a put option to go short on the underlying assets. Just like the call option, this also must have limited downside and unlimited upside potential.

Let us consider the following example where the option profile payoff is shown at long expiration call and put off positions demonstrating how losses are limited to the paid premium. This is only if the directional views you have turns out to be correct. Additionally, the potential profits on an option position may be unlimited and may start to accrue beyond the breakeven point, in which the gains on that position exceeds the paid premiums.

Call Option   Put Option

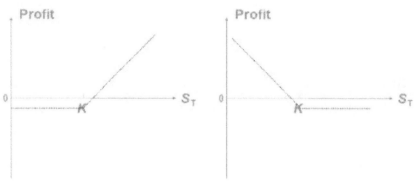

Call and put option payoff profiles with a strike price of K. Source: Surlytrader.com

Step 3 Choose a strike price

One thing that you need to note here is that the strike price of an option plays an essential role in determining its worth. Generally, if the strike price of an option is attractive compared to the current market price for an underlying asset, then the option will have a high cost. Additionally, if the length of time of a particular strike price is long until expiration, then it means that the choice will be expensive.

It is important to note that when the strike price is better that of the existing market, it is considered to be "in the money (ITM)." On the other hand, if it has an ITM strike price, then it means that it has an intrinsic value, which is equal to the difference between existing market price and strike price.

The other thing is that if the strike price of an option is considered right at the existing market, then it is said to be "at the money (ATM)." However, if the level is worse than the current market, then it is "out of money (OTM)." Unlike the ITM, ATM and OTM options do not have an intrinsic value.

What you will realize is that most swing traders seek profits from short-term to intermediate-term directional moves in the market. This means that there is a high likelihood that they will choose an OTM option, which they expect will go into ITM fast for them to sell it back.

The main reason for this is based on the fact that options have a time value as well as an intrinsic value. The time value decays fast as time approached expiration. This, in turn, motivates a swing trader to sell back any options they have bought at the very first opportunity and a reasonable profit presents itself.

Step 4 Decide the expiration date

You may be wondering, but what does an expiration date have to do with starting trading? One thing that you have to note is that the expiration date mirrors the length of time the underlying market is expected to reach your objectives. Generally, you should choose a short-term option if you anticipate that the move will be fast. On the other hand, if you expect that the step will take a longer time, then a long-term option would be ideal.

The last thing you want as a swing trader is selecting an option that expires too soon. This is because it might end up becoming worthless at expiration. Alternatively, you may choose not to buy an option with an expiration date that is too far in the future mainly because of the high cost. You will note that so many swing traders settle for at least a month's options because that offers a sufficient amount of time for your views to pan out before expiration.

Step 5 Time your entry

The entry time for a trade is usually done using technical analysis mainly because traders consider trends and corrections to trends when trading. In most cases, they need to identify the existing trend in the asset they are interested in.

When you are trading with the trend, you must look for a corrective pullback. This will ensure that you are better placed to establish a position in the direction of the pattern. This means that, once the withdrawal loses the momentum, you will be able to tell whether it is the right time for you to step into the market. You can tell when the market is losing momentum by looking at the RSI level in oversold or overbought territories, indicating a divergence in price.

Step 6 Execute your trade

Now, you know whether the time for business is right, then the next thing is for you to execute according your trading plan. For instance, you may opt to purchase OTM call options if the trend is higher compared to OTM put options when the market has a downward trend.

Note that how you trade is as important as where you trade. Therefore, you must ensure that you select the right broker to partner with you during trading. Trust me, when you are frequently trading as a swing trader, the spreads and fees can accumulate over some time, hence the need for a trading partner.

Step 7 Manage the position

Once you execute a trade and have established a reasonable position, it is critical to note that you run the risk of loss. However, since you buy an option, the risk is limited to paid premiums. It is also vital that you watch the underlying market so that you can effectively manage the option trade.

If you buy an OTM option, you can opt to sell it once the underlying market reaches the strike price. This way, it becomes ATM resulting in the choice picking up extra premiums because the value increases. It is critical to note that competing with potential gains serves as the time decay for every full day an option draws nearer to its expiration date.

This means that you will need to sell the position of the option when you first get an opportunity. This way, you avoid having a trade that is based on a directionally sound view that will lose you money as a result of excessive time decay. However, if the market appears like trade, it will eventually pan out, and the short-term move you anticipated to capitalize on fails to materialize. This, in turn, will cause you to consider taking more time for it to come into reality.

The good thing is that you can achieve this by merely executing a calendar roll out for the trade or spread that entails selling back the near-term option so that you can buy a long-term option even though they are of the same strike price. This way, you avoid making losses because of increasing time decay on the near-money option as the date of expiration draws closer.

How To Enter A Trade

This is the most important part of the trade mainly because at this time, your trading capital is at risk. When you have already joined the trade and the stocks go in your favor, then you can relax, manage your stops and wait for a suitable time to exit gracefully.

Here, you will learn the basic price patterns you can use when entering stocks. Once you are familiar with the strategy, you can then proceed into trying advanced trading strategies based on the particular patterns you are trading.

Now, with your entry strategy, the very first thing you need to do is identification of swing points. You may think, "what is a swing point?" Well, this simply refers to a pattern that is made up of three candles.

If you are making entries on long positions, then it is critical that you look for a low swing point. On the other hand, if you are looking for entries on short positions, then you look for high swing points.

But how can you identify a reversal using swing points?

For swing points low, the first candle makes a low, the second makes a lower low, and the third makes a higher low. From this, the third candle simply tells you that the seller is weak and there is a high chance of stock reversals.

In the case of a swing point high, the first candle makes a high, the second makes a higher high and the third makes a lower high. Here, the third candle simply tells you that the buyer has become weaker and there is a chance of stocks reversing.

In the case of a long entry strategy, the main aim here is to find stocks that have already pulled back and made a swing point low.

Let us consider the following example;

At point 1 there is a low, and a lower low is seen at point 2. Finally, a higher low is observed at point 3. This is a classic example of a swing point low and the entry strategy here would be to enter this trade on the day of the third candle.

Now, let us consider a stock on the short side;

Here, the points 1, 2 and 3 represent a high, higher high, and a lower low, respectively. This means that you would enter the trade on the third candle. One thing that is important to note here is that not all swing points result into powerful reversals.

However, of great importance is that for a reversal to happen, there has to be development of a swing point. Therefore, ensure that you take time to review a couple of stock charts to assess all the reversals that have happened in the past. This way, you will be in a position to quickly determine crucial price patterns.

When considering an entry point into the trade, the other factor that you need to look at is the consecutive price patterns. Ideally, you would want to trade stocks that possess consecutive down days before swing point low develops. Well, this would be the best-case scenario. Let us consider the following example on the long side;

What you will note is that this has been reversed on the short side. In such a case, it is paramount that you identify consecutive up days before a swing point high develops.

When looking for development of swing points, what you need to do is look at the left part of the chart to determine if the stocks lie at the support or resistance area. This way, you will improve the reliability of your entry strategy in the trade.

Other times, it is important that you become a little aggressive with your entry using advanced strategies that we will discover later in the book. Now, you are in a better position to know when to enter into a trade, but the question is, how do you know when to exit?

Here, you will need an exit strategy. There are two major questions that you need to ask yourself when identifying an exit strategy;

- Where do you intend to get out of the trade if the stocks do not go in your favor?
- Where do you intend on taking the profits if the stocks do not go in your favor?

Answering these questions will help you consistently make money in the stock market.

Start by setting your initial stop loss order

When you buy stocks, it is critical that you set a stop loss point to protect your capital in case the stocks go against you. There are two kinds, a physical stop loss and a mental stop loss. Well, the physical stop loss simply refers to an order you place with your broker to sell or purchase (if you are short). On the other hand, a mental stop refers to you clicking the sell button in order to exit the trade. Technically, it does not really matter what kind of stop you choose to go with.

One important point to note is that before getting out of the trade, coming up with the right exit strategy is critical. Do you always follow through with your plans? If you are disciplined, then you will always need to exit the trade when your predetermined plan tells you so irrespective of what stop you use.

But where does your initial stop go to? This is where you need a stop that makes sense, and it has to be out of all the stocks' background noise. Consider looking at the stock average range over the last 10 days. If this average is something like $1.1, then your stocks need to be at least this far from the entry price. It is not sensible to have a stop set at $.25 which is far from your entry price, otherwise you will have a premature stop.

If you are trading long positions, the initial stops should go under the support area as well as a swing point low. Therefore, if you are looking for a really easy way to set your initial step, then it is advisable that you set your stop loss below 30 period EMA. Trust me, a strong stock should not further from below this moving average because if it does, then you should be out of the trade already.

Should you use a time stop? When you buy stocks, your expectations are that they go in your favor within a couple of days. However, if they don't, you do not need to keep waiting for them to move in your desired direction. In other words, you will need to sell all your shares so that you can move on to something else.

The last thing you want is tying your trading capital on a stock that is just trading on the sidelines. It is high time you start treating your stocks like an employee. If it does not do what you hired them to do, then the best thing is to fire them.

Go for profit taking strategies

Now that you know how to exit trade when it does not go in your favor, it is important that you know various exit strategies to employ when determining when to take your profits. Trust me, this is the fun part.

Using a trailing stop

This is one of the easiest and unemotional ways of getting out of the trade. If a trade is going to be a typical swing trade with a short holding time of days to few weeks, then you can set your trail stop at 10-15 cents below the previous day's low. Alternatively, you can place it below the current day's low.

If you find a stock at the start of a trend, then it is advisable that you hold it for a longer duration. When you have big winnings all the time, your trading account will keep fattening. Therefore, you can control this by trailing stops below the swing lows until they are all stopped out.

Selling at resistance

When you purchase a pullback, it is important that you look to the left side of the chart to determine your previous swing point high. This is referred to as the first resistance areas the stocks will encounter. Your hope is for the stocks to power through this area. However, if it doesn't, then you sell it.

Selling into strengths

There will come a time when you will want to take some profits and sell them into a powerful rally. One thing that you need to note is that your stocks are prone to a selloff when extended above the 10-period moving average. From the graph, you can see that once bought the pullback, the stocks exploded through the past swing point high, and this is the point where you should take your profits.

What would have happened if you got stopped out? The truth is that you would have lost a huge chunk of your profit. This is why the most sensible thing at this point is to take a portion of your profits off the table.

That said, there is no perfect strategy There are times when you will realize that you sold too soon or too late. This is the bad news. However, the good news is that for you to be successful, you do not necessarily need to have a perfect exit strategy. You just need to protect your money when you are not right so that you can take your profits when you are.

Long Vs. Short Position

We have been referring to short and long and you may be wondering what they really mean. Well, these two refer to two different trading strategies in the stock market.

Remember that the stock market is simply a tag of war between sellers and buyers.

These strategies are an equivalent of bulls and bears used to fight.

It is important that as a trader, you know what strategy to use and when to use it. This does not mean that you have to use both strategies. There are times when you are comfortable with one over the other, and that is perfectly fine.

The type of strategy you choose will depend on whether you intend on opening the trade by selling or buying. You have to know what order you are placing when going short or long. You can simply place a stop loss when making an order so that your position is protected. The thing with stop loss is that they will protect your profits while keeping losses as minimal as possible.

When you decide to go long, the hope is that the price will also go up. If you are day trader, then long and buy are used interchangeably. If you are a new trader, you may think of long as long-term trading. However, the point is that this means that you believe the price is likely to go up.

Because of that, you will hear traders say that they are going long and that does not mean that they are holding stocks for extended durations. They could hold the stocks for just a few minutes, hence the difference between long and short trading.

Note that just because you have insight into trading does not mean that you should go out and copy every trader out there. It is important that you do your due diligence and you may see a different play on the stock. You do not need margins to do long trading. The bottom line should be having funds to cover all the trades.

So, what is short trading?

Shorting simply means selling shares you do not own so that you can buy them back when the prices go down. In other words, you are borrowing shares from your broker with the hope that the prices will fall. This way, you are covering your position to close it out and give back the shares to the broker.

The difference between the price where you sold and covered is what makes your profit. Well, you have to realize that shorting is a really risky business. This is mainly because you may lose an infinite amount of money in the process.

If your stocks trade to $0 and you are long, the unfortunate thing is that you lose your initial investment. The good thing is that it cannot go negative, hence you will not lose much more than your investment.

However, if you go short and the stocks keep moving up rather than going down, chances are that you might end up losing everything and some. Well, this does not result from risk management and stop losses. The secret is for you to keep your losses minimal. If a trade goes against that, it is advisable that you get out of it rather than holding on with the hope of recovering losses. This is especially the case when you are shorting.

Realize that not all brokers will allow short selling. Therefore, if you are interested in short selling, it is critical that you ensure that your broker has options. If not, then it is better that you look into other brokers like interactive brokers.

How can you tell whether to go short or long? The most important thing here is for you to see patterns. Candlesticks will tell you a story and when grouped together, they form a pattern that will offer you support, resistance and direction to move.

If you trade without patterns, then know that you are setting yourself up for disaster!

The bottom-line is to "always aim at cutting your losses fast and take your profits."

Chapter 1: How To Forecast Price Directions Using Technical Analysis

Background (Charles Dow)

You may be wondering who Charles Dow truly is. Well, this is one of the oldest forefathers behind technical analysis. This is where the Dow theory comes from with all the basic tenets that guides swing trading.

The Dow theory was developed through the 1851-1902 period. That said, one thing that you have to note is that these set of principles were not viewed by Dow as a set. Instead, he thought of them as ways that play a central role in enhancing one's perception of the market. Considering the fact that they were written over a century ago, it is important for you as a trader to bring in your modern interpretation of the rules to suit the situation prevailing in the market.

Traditionally, there are two major ways in which you can perceive the market namely; technical method and the fundamental method. When it comes to swing trading, the fundamental method goes a long way in largely interpreting the economic news as well as long-term trading.

There are so many traders around the world who interpret changes in macroeconomic policies all across the globe. In fact, most of them often rely largely on speculations.

However, the case of technical analysis is rather pragmatic. This is mainly because it concerns itself with indicators that serve as tools traders can use when forecasting prices. Speculation has never been easier!

The trick is starting by opening a trading platform and keying in some indicators on the chart. The next thing is for you to buy and sell when the indicators direct you to. When you apply the right money management techniques you increase your chances of making money. However, there is more to trading than just that!

In other words, you will need to understand the reasons why the market moves in the manner in which it moves. There are so many renowned traders who have in the past tried to place an order in the chaotic moves happening in the market. However, there is none of them that has been successful in influencing the market moves like

Charles Dow did. To date, the Dow theory holds the key to the market like no other.

Basics Of Technical Analysis

There are various tenets to technical analysis in swing trading. These include;

A. The market has three movements

If you ask any trend follower, one thing they will tell you is that there are various trends within a wide range of timeframes. In such an instance, an hourly uptrend would possibly be discounted by a downtrend on a weekly chart. The ability to differentiate between various timeframe movements is critical.

According to the Dow theory, there are three movements;

Major trend

This is also referred to as the primary movement. It is a long-term trend that Dow explains that it runs from a period of less than a year to several years. however, one thing that you need to bear in mind here is that you can look at it from a long-term point of view based on what the weekly and monthly charts reveal.

Medium swing

This is also referred to as the secondary reaction or the intermediate reaction. Unlike the major trend that is long-term, this is a medium-term movement. In other words, it is anything that runs from a period of ten days to about 3 months. Think of it as a view extracted from a daily chart or a 4-hour chart.

Minor movement

This is also referred to as short swing. It is a short-term movement that is often taken over a period of a few hours to a month period. In such a case, it is ideal and sensible to use an hourly chart among other lower timeframe charts.

B. Trends have three phases

These phases include;

Accumulation phase

This is where "in-the-know" investors are involved in actively building new positions or exiting positions against the opinion that the general market holds at the time. At this point, the stock prices do not change much at this point based on the fact that this opinion goes against the grain. Hence, there are so many buyers out there that have the ability of making up for any selling and vice versa.

Participation

In this phase, once the market catches on to the "in-the-know" investors, you will be able to see a very sharp reversal in the market. At this point, you will realize that technical traders begin to participate in the trade.

Panic

In this phase, once you see the rampant trader's speculation catching on and taking hold, the "in-the-know" investors start reversing their position as they approach the end of the trend.

C. The stock market discounts all news

This principle simply states that a stock price often mirrors the underlying economics and financial situation from the time all this news is publicly available.

D. Stock market averages must serve as a confirmation for each other

Have you ever thought about the importance of the US rail network in shipping goods throughout the entire country? Have you ever thought about the reason behind its success?

Well, the Dow Transportation Index played a significant role in growth of the economic activity. In fact, so many factories throughout the country contributed to the rise of the rail use, something that is uniquely tied to the Dow Jones days than it is today.

That said, the Dow's idea went a long way in ensuring the confirmation between two stock indices, something that still holds value today. According to Charles Dow, when the two indices moved in the same direction, it was an indication of a greater confidence compared to when there is a divergence between the two indices.

Therefore, it is quite sensible to look for a confirmation using the case of whether both indices drive higher lows or higher highs when there is an uptrend. Today, there is need for traders to identify alternative markets. However, one thing that is important to note is that this notion is strongly correlated to the markets in finding confirmation, something that still holds so much value.

E. Trends are often confirmed by volumes

According to Dow theory, volume plays a very critical role as a tool used in the confirmation or refuting of a market move. For instance, when the market is moving on low volumes, it simply means that there are quite a number of possible things that could happen.

One of the main reasons here is that there may be an overly aggressive buyer or seller whose intention is to move the market. However, you have to realize that when there are significant price movements, they are linked with high volumes. According to Dow, this is exactly what gives a "true" view of the market.

F. Trends exist unless proved otherwise

It is important to note that markets do not by any means move in a straight line. With several fundamental events taking place, there is so much volatility this offers, hence, there will be times when the trends will push things under so much pressure.

However, according to Dow, the trends are expected to remain in play even in the midst of so much "noise" in the market. This means that the trend needs to be given the benefit of the doubt when such retracements are taking place. The only thing is that Dow does not offer specific ways in which the trends can be reversed or even a way to know when it's just a retracement move.

That said, there are several other rules you can extend to suit the plethora of trading situations for you in the modern world of trading. Starting from the new-based trading to correlated markets and recognition trends among others, the Dow theory plays a significant role in creating a strong backbone of several technical analysis courses globally. When you have a strong knowledge of these rules/principles as a trader, you will get on the right footing with all of your trades.

Welcome aboard!

Underlying Assumption Of Technical Analysis

Two primary methods exist that play a significant role in analyzing securities and in making investment decisions. These methods are what we have just mentioned in the sections above; fundamental and technical analysis.

Just as a recap, fundamental analysis essentially involves analyzing the financial statements of a company. The main aim of doing this analysis is to determine what the fair values of the business is. On the other hand, technical analysis simply assumes that the price of security mirrors all information available publicly and instead chooses to pay attention on statistics of price movements. The main aim of technical analysis is to try and shed light into all the sentiments the market holds on price trends by focusing on the trends and patterns instead of the analyzing attributes of securities.

There are so many editorials released by Charles Dow shedding light into the theory of technical analysis. In these writings, there are two major assumptions he made;

1. The markets are efficient as long as the values that represent factors influencing security prices are there.
2. But, the movements of market prices are not exactly random as many people think. Instead, they possess a trend and pattern of movement that tends to repeat itself over time.

It is these two major assumptions that form the framework for technical analysis trading.

Ever heard of Efficient market hypothesis (EMH)? Well, this simply means the prevailing market price of a security at any time mirrors all available information with a high degree of accuracy. This simply means that it represents the actual fair value if the security.

You may be thinking what this assumption is based on. the truth is that this assumption follows the idea that the market price has the tendency of mirroring the total knowledge participants in the market possess.

While this assumption is said to be true, news announcements about securities with either short- or long-term influence have the tendency of causing a shift in their market price. Of importance to note is that technical analysis only works when and if the markets are weakly efficient.

The other basic assumption that underlies technical analysis is based off of the notion that price changes do not just happen randomly. In fact, they do not just lead to the belief of technical analysis marketing trends whether in the short- or long-term. It assumes that these changes can be identified so that the trader's in the market have the opportunity to make profits from their investments on the basis of analyzing trends.

Today, there are three major assumptions of technical analysis;

Assumption 1: The market has the tendency of discounting everything

It is quite unfortunate that most experts criticize technical analysis because of the fact that it ignores fundamental factors and instead chooses to focus on price movements. According to technical analysts, such factors as the company's fundamentals, market psychology and broad market factors play a central role in contributing to the stock prices.

In other words, this simply eliminates the need to consider these factors one at a time when making an investment decision. This means that the only thing that remains in the price movement analysis, something that technical analysts perceive as the result of supply and demand for a given stock in the market.

Assumption 2: Price moves in trends

According to technical analysts, price moves often can be short-, medium- or longterm in relation to trend. What this means is that the price of stocks is likely to hold on to past trends rather than moving in an erratic manner. The thing is that most technical trading strategies are often based off of this assumption.

Assumption 3: History often have the tendency if repeating itself over and over again

This is something that technical analysts tend to strongly believe in. It is often thought that the recurrent price movements are because of market psychology, something that tends to be predictable considering the fact that it arises from such emotional feelings as excitement and fear.

In the case of technical analysis, you have to utilize such tools as chart patterns in analyzing such emotions and market movements in order to get deeper insight on market trends. While there are so many forms of technical analysis that has been used in the past, they are still considered to be relevant mainly because they not only capture price movement patterns, but also those that keep repeating themselves.

Chartering The Market

There are a wide range of tools you can use to chart the market. Some of these charts include;

Candlesticks

These are technical tools that often represents data from a wide range of time frames into one price bar. Because of this, they are more useful compared to traditional open-high, low-close bars. They are even better than simple lines connected with dots representing closing prices.

The thing with candlesticks is that they form a pattern that plays a significant role in predicting the direction prices take once complete. With proper color coding, candlestick charts are able to add an in-depth understanding of what they represent such as bearish dark clouds, three black crows, and evening stars among others.

The most important question however is whether the candlestick patterns are reliable or not. Well, the truth is that not all candlestick patterns work as well. It is because of their increasing popularity that their reliability keeps coming down mainly because they have been deconstructed by algorithms and hedge funds.

Such well-funded plays depend on lighting-speed kind of execution when trading against retail investors as well as traditional fund managers who are well known to execute various technical analysis strategies contained in popular texts. In other words, such managers utilize software to trap a large number of participants interested in high-odds bearish and bullish outcomes.

However, the most important point to note is that you will see reliable patterns appear, hence allowing both long- and short-term opportunities for traders to make profits. With the following candlestick patterns, you can easily perform exceptional analysis of the direction and momentum of market prices.

Each one of the following candlestick patterns work within the context of its surrounding price bars when making predictions on higher or lower prices. The other point to note is that they are time-sensitive in two major ways. First, they only operate within the chart's limitations irrespective of whether it is intraday, daily, weekly, or monthly. Secondly, once the pattern is complete, its potency tends to decline fast at least 3-5 bars.

Candlestick patterns

The candlestick analysis relies hugely on the works of Thomas Bulkowski. The principle here is based on two expected pattern outcomes; continuation and reversal. The main role of the candlestick reversal pattern is to offer predictions in relation to change in the direction of prices. On the other hand, the continuation patterns play a significant role in predicting an extension in the existing direction of market prices.

The black candlestick on the other hand represents a closing print that is way lower compared to the opening print.

Some of the most common candlestick patterns you are likely to encounter include;

Three-line strike

This is a bullish three-line strike reversal pattern that brings out three black candles on the downtrend. On each bar, you will observe a lower low and the closing is closer to the intra-bar low.

Additionally, the fourth bar opens lower. However, it reverses hugely on the outside bar closing above the high registered by the very first candle in the series. It is also important to note that the opening print marks a low on the fourth bar, which according to Bulkowski, it predicts higher prices at an accuracy level of 84%.

Two black gapping

This is a bearish continuation pattern that often has been shown to appear after top in the uptrend. It is characterized by a gap down that gives rise two black bars that post lower lows. It is this pattern that plays a central role in predicting whether the decline is going to continue to lower lows, something that would perhaps trigger a downtrend on a broader scale. Based on Bulkowski's analysis, this pattern is key in predicting lower prices with an accuracy of about 68%.

Three black crows

This is a reversal pattern that begins near the high of an uptrend. It is characterized by three black bars that post lower lows closing near the intra-bar lows. The three black crow pattern plays a central role in predicting whether a decline will continue to the point of lower lows hence triggering a broader scale on the downtrend.

One thing that is important to note is that the most bearish version of this pattern begins at a new high. This is mainly because it aims at trapping buyers into joining momentum plays. Based on Bulkowski's analysis, it is with the help of this pattern that a trader can tell when lower prices are likely to happen with a 78% rate of accuracy.

Evening star

This is also a reversal pattern that begins with a tall white bar, which is responsible for carrying an uptrend to a new high. On the next bar, you will notice that the market gap in such a pattern is higher. However, you will not see an appearance of fresh buyers, something that in turn gives rise to a narrow range candlestick.

On the third bar, you will notice that there is a gap down, which completes the pattern. This bar is responsible for telling a trader that the decline will keep on to lower lows, hence triggering a broader scale on the downtrend. Based on Bulkowski's analysis, it is this kind of pattern that goes a long way in predicting lower prices with an accuracy of about 72%.

Abandoned baby

This is a bullish reversal pattern that is known to appear on a downtrend's low, once several black candles have printed lower lows. On the next bar, you will notice that the market gap becomes lower. However, there is no appearance of fresh sellers, something that gives rise to a narrow range Doji candlestick that has opening and closing prints at the same price.

On the third bar is a bullish gap that completes the pattern. This predicts that the recovery will keep on to higher highs. This is what will trigger a broader scale on the uptrend. Based on Bulkowski's analysis, it is this pattern that goes a long way in predicting higher prices with an accuracy level of 70%.

That said, it is important to bear in mind that the candlestick pattern is critical in capturing the attention of market players. However, so many continuation and reversal signals that are emitted by these patterns often fail to work reliably when applied in the modern electronic surrounding.

The good thing is that the statistics given by Bulkowski reveal an unusual level of accuracy for these pattern's narrow selection, something that in turn offers traders actionable signals to sell and buy.

It is important that you use all the insights you have gained from the candlestick pattern when investing in asset-based stocks that require a brokerage account. Therefore, it is important that you identify the best online broker that is right for you and will meet all your investment needs.

Bar charts

Overtime, you will notice that bar charts show multiple price bars. Each of the bars will show you how prices mover over a specific period of time. If daily, then you will be able to see how prices are moving every single day.

One thing that you will notice is that each bar will typically show open, high, low, and close prices for a given period of time. The good news is that you can also adjust so that you can only see high, low, and close prices.

With technical analysts, a bar chart, among other charts such as candlesticks and line charts are useful in helping them monitor the performance of asset prices, which is critical in helping them make informed decisions. In other words, a bar chart plays a central role in helping a trader analyze trends, monitor price movements/volatility, and detect possible reversal in trends.

How does a bar chart work?

Well, a bar chart simply refers to a collection of price bars. Each bar on the chart represents the manner in which prices are moving over a given period of time. You will notice that each of the bars possess a vertical line showing the highest price attained for a certain duration as well as the lowest price attained during that period.

One thing that you need to note is that the opening price is often marked by a small horizontal line on the left side of the vertical line. On the other hand, the closing price is marked by a small horizontal line that lies on the right side of the vertical line.

If under certain conditions the closing price is higher than the opening price, you will notice that the bar will be colored black or green. However, if the closing price is lower than the opening price, it demonstrates that the price declined during that time and hence will be marked red in color.

Understand that color coding the price bars is something that is dependent on the direction of price movement; either higher or lower. This is something that goes a long way in helping you as a trader to see the trend in price movements in a very clear manner. The good news is that most charting platforms offer these color-coding options.

As an investor or trader, it is your responsibility to decide which period you would be interested in analyzing. If you have a one-minute bar chart, that would show new price movements by the minute, which are useful if you are a day trader rather than an investor. On the other hand, a weekly bar chart will show new price movement bars, which best suit a long-term investor instead of a day trader.

How do you interpret bar charts?

Considering the fact that bar charts demonstrate open, high, low, and close prices for every period, there are lots of information that you can analyze as a trader or an investor.

When you see a long vertical bar, this is an indicator that there are large price differences between the low and high periods. This simply means that the volatility increased during this time. On the other hand, if the chart has small vertical bars, it is an indicator that there was minimal volatility.

If there is a large distance between the close and open prices, then it simply means that there was a significant price move. On the other hand, if the close was far much above the open, it indicates that buyers were far active during this period, indicating more possibility of buying in future. If the close is too close to the open, it may indicate that there was a certain conviction in price moves during that period.

It is important to note that you can draw valuable information from the location of the close with regard to the high and the low. In other words, if an assert rallied way higher during this period and the close was below the high, it indicates that as you approached the end of the period, sellers came in. This simply means that it is less bullish compared to if the asset closed nearer to its high for that period.

If you have the bar chart color coded on the basis of price rise or fall during a given trading period, then you can draw so much information from just looking at the colors. For instance, if you see a green or black bar, then you know that it is an uptrend that indicates a strong upward price movement. On the other hand, if the price bars are colored red, then this is typical of a downtrend, indicating a strong downward movement in price.

Bar charts versus candlesticks

Did you know that bar charts are quite similar to the Japanese candlestick charts? These two types of charts give us information in different ways.

In other words, when you look at a bar chart, there are so many vertical lines with small horizontal lines both on the right and left side of the chart, which indicate open and close prices. On the other hand, candlesticks do have vertical lines that indicate what the high and low of a period are.

However, the major difference between the close and open is the fact that they are often marked by thicker portions referred to as real body. If the close is below the open, then you will notice that the body is shaded in or colored red. If the close is above the open, then you will see that the body is white or colored green. While the information drawn from both charts is the same, the visual outlooks differ significantly.

Let us consider a bar chart in the SPDR S&P 500 ETF. When there is a decline, you will notice that the bars get longer. This indicates that there is an increase in price volatility. What you have to note is that declines are often marked by a more down in the price bars indicated by the red colors, compared to when there is an up in price bars indicated by the green color.

Takeaway message

> A bar chart tells us the open, high, low, and close prices for a given duration
>
> The vertical lines represented on the price bars indicate the low and high prices for a given duration
>
> The right and left horizontal lines on each of the bars are indicators of close and open prices
>
> Bar charts are often color coded and if the close is above the open, then this is indicated by a green or black color. If the close is below the open, then the bars will be marked by the red colors.

Price Action And Psychology

One of the advantages of price action is the fact that it is hugely flexible and can be applied through a wide range of techniques. You can restructure, modify and test it using various programming skills.

In such a case, price action is not only a discretionary trading technique but also an aspect that you can fine-tune based on your ideology. Therefore, note that you can come up with your own strategies simply using price actions to suit your trading style, personality, and many more traits.

Apart from the fact that price action can be discretionary, it can also be systematic. This is what adds a whole new dimensional advantage over other indicators. In this case, we will get more insight on how price action impacts market psychology by simply using a clear chart without any other indicators.

So, the question is, what is price action?

Well, you can simply define price action as the use of natural price movements in the market when analyzing and trading. In other words, you make all your trading decisions on the basis of price bars on an indicator-free/naked price chart.

The price movements you observe on a market's price chart are often created by all economic variables. Irrespective of whether the economic variables are filtered down by computer or human trader, the movement that is created will be observed on a price chart.

Therefore, rather than attempting to analyze millions of economic variables every day, you can choose to learn trading from price action analysis. This is mainly because when you employ this style, you ensure that you are making use of all market variables by trading off of the price action that is created by the market variables.

So, what is market psychology?

Every particular time, the market is experiencing such sentiments as greed, circumstances, and expectations, all of which contribute to the overall mentality of investing groups.

Just like a human being, the market demonstrates a wide range of behaviors and attitudes based on the existing situation or scenario. Some of these include panic, fear, euphoria, greed, and many more. By just reading a price chart, you can understand the behavior a market exhibits, which will help you to anticipate what the market is likely to do in future.

How do you read the market psychology through price action?

One thing that is important to note is that the price action offers a trader an open window to look through the market so as to understand its psychology. Well, this is not something simple in the very beginning. The good thing is that it is not impossible! Just like any other skill, you will have to be willing to learn it overtime and experience.

To read the market psychology through price action, you have to start by opening a clear chart and then taking out all indicators therein. Secondly, start marking the chart whenever you deem necessary by just employing your intuition. Thirdly, attempt to put yourself in the state of the market and start thinking about the kind of move to make. Finally, use your intuitions to anticipate the next move.

Understand that the lower time frames will offer you so much exposure to patterns. However, in such a case, the time spent contemplating is greatly reduced. What is most important is for you to select a time frame that will permit you to commit to the exercise. When you do this for a couple of days and then give up, then you will have wasted time. Trust me, it is important that you do not underestimate the power of a simple charting exercise.

When trying to read the market psychology, it is critical that you study the volumes. If they are high, then it is an indication that the traders are quite unlucky and will be losing money in their positions. They will feel the sharp sting of the losses they will make.

To alleviate this kind of pain, traders will begin to close down their positions. As they exit the market, a trend based on the high volume will potentially be short-lived.
However, if the trend is based on moderate volume, it can last for a very long time.

This is because losses will accumulate over time and become significantly large.

Some of the market psychology indicators include;

1. On-balance Volume (OBV)

This is an indicator that was devised by someone called Joseph Granville. This refers to a running total that is known to fall or rise on every trading day depending on whether prices close lower or higher that day compared to the previous one.

OBV is usually considered to be one of the leading indicators of market psychology mainly because it falls or rises just prior to actual prices catching on. When you see a new OBV high, then this shows the power of bulls, weaknesses of bears and possibly the resulting increase in prices.

On the other hand, when you see a new OBV low, this is an indicator of an opposite pattern in which the bears are powerful while the bulls are weak, hence a potential decline in price value. When there is a signal that differs from that of actual prices, then it means that the market volumes are not consistent with the actual prices. A price shift can possibly alleviate such an imbalance.

2. Accumulation/Distribution (A/D)

This is also one of the leading market indicators that relates to volume. However, this particular factor considers both opening and closing prices. When you have a positive A/D, this indicates that the prices were higher at the closing compared to opening. On the other hand, when the A/D value is negative, it is vice versa.

In this case, the bear and bull winners are credited with just a fraction of the day's volume based on the range and distance there is between the closing and opening prices. The obvious thing is that when there is a wide range between the closing and the opening, it is a stronger A/D signal. However, the most important thing is the pattern of the A/D highs and lows.

If a market is shown to open higher and close lower, this causes the A/D to decline. This is what causes the upward-trending market to be weaker than it was at the very beginning.

The importance of the A/D signal depends on the insight it offers into various activities of distinct groups of amateur and professional traders. The thing is that amateur traders are often found to have a high likelihood of influencing the market's opening prices. The amateur traders often base their first trades on such things as financial and corporate news they read overnight or are issued by their favorite companies once the market shuts down.

One thing that you have to realize is that as the trade wears on, professionals are in a better position to determine the ultimate results of the day. If amateurs disagree with professionals, chances are that professionals will drive the prices lower for the sake of closing.

However, when the advantages are more bullish compared to amateurs, it is these advantages that will cause the prices to rise throughout the day up to the close. The activities of professional traders are viewed to be more important than that of amateur traders.

3. Open interest

The other major indicator of market psychology is that of open interest, which applies to future markets. It is an indicator of how the future contracts will read as well as other options that expire at a later date in the future.

The main role of open interest is to add total long and short contracts into the market on a certain day. The absolute value that is derived from this addition is considered to correspond to a cumulative short and long position.

Note that open interest only falls and rises whenever there is a new contract created or destroyed. In other words, one short and long seller has to join the market for the open interest to increase. On the other hand, one short and long sellers have to close their positions for the fall of open interest to happen.

When the open interest deviates from the norm, then interest (pun intended) in it increases. In such a case, an absolute value is not of much interest. It is the open interest that goes a long in mirroring the market psychology through the inherent conflict between bears and bulls.

In order for you to move the open interest up or down, it is important that both the bears and the bulls show confidence in their long and short positions. When there is rise in the open interest, it indicates that the bulls are confident in getting into a contract with the bears. On the other hand, the bears have to demonstrate their confidence in their bearishness to get into that position.

However, when this happens, you have to bear in mind that one group will definitely have to lose. But as long as the loser enters into the binding contract, the fall or rise of the open interest will still remain. That said, you have to note that there is more to the open interest indicator than meets the eye!

How do you read the open interest signals?

First it is important to understand that the open interest points at an increase in the number of traders that will potentially lose. This is what plays a central role in propelling the trend forward. An open interest that tends to rise when there is an uptrend simply reveals that a certain number of bears strongly believe in that the market is way too high. However, if the uptrend increases, chances are that their positions will be squeezed causing their purchase to propel the market higher.

On the other hand, if the open interest remains constant when there is an uptrend in the market, this indicates that there has been stoppage in the supply of losers. This is mainly because those who are coming into the market are previous buyers whose aim is to make profits from their existing positions. In such a case, there is a likelihood that the uptrend is coming to an end.

When there is a downtrend, shorts aggressively sell as the participants purchasing become bottom pickers. What is even more interesting is that value investors begin to exit their positions as soon as prices begin to drop causing the prices to be even lower.

If in a declining market, the open interest goes up, this will cause the downtrend to continue. However, if the open interest stays constant, chances are that the remaining bottom pickers become few and those that are available for the contracts are additional bears that short earlier and would like to cover before exiting the market.

The bears that exit leave the market with profits often trigger a flat open interest in the downtrend. This means that the best gains one will draw from the downtrend will likely have been realized already.

Finally, when the open interest is falling, it is an indication that losers are leaving their positions as winners take profits. It also demonstrates that there are no additional losers to assume the position of those who have already given up.

When there is a falling open interest, it is a clear signal that winners get to enjoy profits while losers lose (pun intended) hope. Losing a contract is directly linked with the drawing near of the end of a trend.

That said, you have to bear in mind that there are times when reading the market trends and the market psychology is effective especially when using certain metrics. However, when you exercise care while selecting the indicators to use, take time to understand their limitations, and then apply them in a holistic manner, you will be better placed to gauge the market's mood and make changes win your position where necessary.

Technical Indicator Tools For Directions

Have you ever wondered what some of the technical indicators are available for you to use in trading? Do you already have some in mind? Do you have any idea how to use them in trading?

In this section, we will delve deeper into the 7 popular indicators you can use to profit from their signals. Just as a recap, technical trading is about reviewing charts so that you can make decisions based on pertinent indicators and patterns.

In the previous section, we have seen how you can use such patterns as candlesticks and bar charts in deriving information on where prices are likely to move next. Understand that technical trading indicators serve as overlays or additions on the charts whose main aim is to offer extra set of information on prices and volumes by way of mathematical calculations.

Some of these technical indicators include;

Indicator #1: Price trends

One important thing that you need to understand about price trend indicators is the act that they predict the direction in which the market is moving. In some instances, they are referred to as oscillators mainly because just like a wave, they have a tendency of moving between high and low values.

Some of the trend indicators of importance include; Parabolic SAR, Parts of the

Ichimoku Kinko Hyo, as well as moving average convergence divergence (MACD).

Ichimoku Kinko Hyo

This is also referred to as the Ichimoku cloud. It simply refers to a collection of lines that are plotted on a chart. They are critical in measuring future price momentum as well as determining areas of resistance and support in the future.

At first, you may be tempted to think of this indicator as a very complex phenomenon. However, here is a simpler breakdown of the same that will help you to better understand what it stands for;

> **Kijun Sen**: This is simply the blue line. It is also referred to as the base line or the standard line. It is calculated by simply averaging the lowest low and the highest high over the past 26 periods.

> **Senkou span:** This is represented by the green and red band. The very first senkou line is simply calculated by getting an average of the Tenkan Sen and the Kijun Sen and then plotting 26 periods forward.

The second Senkou line is obtained by simply averaging the lowest low and the highest high over a span of 52 periods, and then plotting it 26 periods ahead.

Tenkan Sen: is represented by the red line and is often referred to as the turning line. It is often derived from an average of lowest lows and highest highs over a span of 9 periods that have passed.

Chikou Span: is represented by the green line. It is also referred to as the lagging line. Today, it is considered as the closing price that is plotted at least 26 periods behind.

Consider the following graph;

The most important question that you need to answer at this point is how can you translate these lines to make trading profits?

Well, one thing that you need to understand is that the Senkou span serves a critical role as a dynamic support as well as offering some level of resistance. In other words, if the price is above this span, then the line that lies above it acts as a first line support while the one below it is the second line of support. On the other hand, if the prices lie below the span, then the line that is at the bottom is the first line of resistance while the one above it is the second line of resistance.

Consider the following graph;

Now, the Kijun Sen represented by the blue line is often useful when confirming the price trends. In other words, if there is a price breakout above the Kijun Sen, chances are that it will rise higher. On the other hand, if there is a decline in price below this blue line, chances are that they will drop even lower.

Thirdly, the red line (Tenkan Sen) also plays a similar role as the Kijun Sen in the confirmation of price trends. If there is an up and down movement of this line, then it is an indication that the market is trending. However, if the line seems to be moving sideways, chances are that the market is ranging.

Consider the following example;

The first graph represents a flat Tenkan Sen while the one below is a downward Tenkan Sen that represents a downtrend.

One thing that is important to remember at all times is that the red line is a price trend indicator. On the other hand, the Chikou span represented by the green line is often plotted at least 26 periods behind the existing period.

Therefore, when the line crosses the price in a bottom-up orientation, chances are that the price will go up. However, when the line crosses the price in a top-down orientation, this is an indication that the there is a high likelihood of prices declining.

Consider the following example;

That said, it is important that you always remember what each line represents. This is because, if you begin to mix up the Kijun Sen and the Chikou span, chances are that you will confuse when a downtrend and uptrend are happening and this might cost you lots of losses that will kill your trading account!

Moving average convergence divergence (MACD)

This is also a trend indicator that consists of a slow line, fast line and a histogram. This is where you grab a cup of coffee if you have not had any yet! Trust me, you need that coffee because things can get a little confusing here.

For this particular indicator, some of the inputs that you need include slower moving average (MA-slow), fast-moving average (MA-fast), and a number that plays a role in defining the period during which the next average will happen (MA-period).

One thing that is important to note is that the MACD slow line simply refers to the moving average of the MACD fast line. Here, the number of periods is often dependent on the MA period. On the other hand, MACD fast line refers to the moving average of the difference between MA fast and MA slow.

Take a minute to let these concepts sink in!

Now, what about the histogram? Well, the role of the histogram is to demonstrate to us the difference between MACD slow and fast lines.

If you do not get this the first time, you do not have to worry too much. We will work on an example together. Now, let us say that you have MACD 12, 26 and 9. This simply means that the first line is the moving average of the difference between period 12 and period 26 moving averages.

On the other hand, think of the slow line as a 9-period moving average of the fast line while the histogram is the difference between all the MACD lines.

You be wondering what this convergence divergence is all about. To answer that, start by thinking of the histogram as well as the moving averages plotted on separate charts. What you will notice is that the lines cross over from time to time as shown in the figure below;

One thing that is important to note is that as the line difference becomes smaller and smaller, they tend to eventually converge. As the difference between the lines get bigger and bigger, there is a divergence. These features are what you need to look out for when trading.

Now, how do you know when a new trend is forming? The truth is that you can tell this when the MACD lines converge and crossover, indicating that that there is a reverse in the trend. At this point, the lines then begin to diverge. At the point of crossover you will realize that the histogram disappears since the difference between the MACD lines becomes 0.

Consider the following graph;

From the graph above, you will notice that the fast line marked by blue color crossed over the slow orange line around 19th February. What this means is that the downtrend has finally come to an end marking the beginning of an uptrend. What is even interesting is that there was an uptrend for a couple of days with approximately 200,000 pip moves and a whopping $2k profits to make for every Bitcoin!

That said, MACD is composed of moving averages of other moving averages. What this means is that it lags behind price many times and might not be the best indicator to employ when intending to join trends early. However, you can use it when confirming trends.

Parabolic stop and reverse (SAR)

Now, let's move on to something that is a little easier to understand; the parabolic SAR. This is also a trend indicator. What you will notice are dots placed above or below the price, indicating what the potential direction of price movement is likely to be.

Published on TradingView.com, March 25, 2018 15:38 UTC
COINBASE:BTCUSD, 240 8481.26 ▼ -50.06 (-0.59%) O:8421.99 H:8630.00 L:8401.00 C:8481.26

You may be wondering how such a simple indicator is used when trading. Well, the truth is that once the dots are above the price, it indicates that the market is on a downtrend. What this means is that you should be short. If the dots are below the price, then it indicates that the market is in an uptrend. This means that you should be long.

Published on TradingView.com, March 23, 2018 13:20 UTC
BITFINEX:BTCUSD, 240 8330.3 ▼ -369.0 (-4.24%) O:8512.9 H:8516.9 L

One thing that you need to be aware of is that you should not use the Parabolic SAR when operating in a ranging market. In other words, stay away from this indicator when prices are moving sideways. This is because there will be so much noise and chances are that the flips will begin to move side-to-side without necessarily offering you clarity in any signal. However, if you are looking to have an upper hand in strong trends, then parabolic SAR is the best way to go!

Indicator #2: Momentum

With momentum indicators, you get to know how strong a trend is and whether there is a likelihood of a reversal happening. You can therefore use this indicator when selecting top and bottom prices.

Some of the most useful momentum indicators include Relative strength index (RSI), Average directional index (ADX) and Stochastic among others.

Relative strength index (RSI)

This is often plotted on a separate scale. You will notice a single line that is scaled from 0 all through to 100. This plays a central role in identifying both oversold and overbought conditions in the prevailing market. When you read a value >70, this indicates that there has been an overbought in the market while a value <30 indicates an oversold market.

So, how can you make money?

Well, the idea of underlying RSI is for you to select the tops and bottoms when joining a market during trend reversal. This is how you can fully leverage the whole move. Let us consider the chart below;

What do you notice happening around 6th February? Well, the truth is that at this point, the market was oversold. What this means is that it is a strong buy signal for you as a trader. If you had bought the market at this point and then held on to RSI > 70, then you would have 490,000 pips, which is equivalent to around $5,000/Bitcoin.

You can also use RSI when confirming trends. If it is above 50, chances are that the market is in an uptrend. Conversely, if it is <50, then it may indicate that the market is in a downtrend.

In the chart above, RSI tells us that the market was in an oversold condition, something that appeared like a good buy. However, this eventually turned out to be a fake-out as shown in the chart below;

At first, you will realize that the price started going up but the truth is that RSI did not break through the 50-level mark by 4th February, explaining what happened after.

The market simply dropped like a stone starting from $6,000 to way below this value.

If you are someone who is risk-averse, then the most sensible thing for you to do is to wait for a trend confirmation. Yes, this is a trade-off between two major things where on one hand you stand to make lots of profits while on the other you lose lots of pips to the stop! Alternatively, you can choose to wait for confirmation of an uptrend, which means that you will miss out on a huge chunk of profits.

That said, everything will depend on your risk disposition. Ask yourself whether you are willing to accept small losses or take a few big wins. It is only you that can make that decision. My job here is to offer you with the right tools of the trade but it is upon you to decide how to use them.

Indicator #3: Volume

This simply tells you how volume is changing over time. In other words, it tells how much a unit of bitcoin is being sold and bought as time goes by. This is something that plays a significant role since as price changes, the volume tells you how strong the move is.

When you have a bullish move on high volume, there is a high chance that they will be maintained compare to those on low volumes.

Indicator #4: Volatility

The volatility indicators play a central role in revealing to you how much prices are changing over a certain duration. It is a very important market component that without it you may not have a way to make money. In other words, if you are going to make a profit, then you will need the prices to move.

When the level of volatility is high, the prices will change so fast. However, you need to note that this indicator does not tell you anything about the direction in which the prices are moving. It only tells you the price ranges!

When there is low volatility, this indicates that there is a small price move while a high volatility level reveals a big price move. Additionally, a high level of volatility indicates that there is an inefficiency in the market prices.

You may be thinking, but why are these indicators important in the first place?

The truth is that these indicators go a very long way in giving you an idea of the direction prices might go next. This is exactly what you are looking for as a trader so that you can position yourself to leverage the market move and make profits.

It is your responsibility as a trader to understand where the market is going so that you are better prepared for any eventualities. Does this mean that you have to know exactly where the market is going? No. You will never have a certainty of where the market is going. However, you will understand various possibilities and be better positioned for any one of them that materializes.

You have to remember that so many traders make money in both bull and bear markets. This is mainly because they know how to take advantage of both the long and short positions. Therefore, ensure that you do not get too attached to the market directions. As long as the prices in the market are moving, so will you also make profits and these indicators will see to it that you do.

Trend Following Vs. Trading Ranges

Trend trading

This is a method that is often designed to leverage uptrends downtrends, where prices tend to make new highs or prices make new lows, respectively. Additionally, when traders are trend trading, they look at the trendlines, technical indicators and moving averages to determine the direction of the trend. This potentially provides the trade signals.

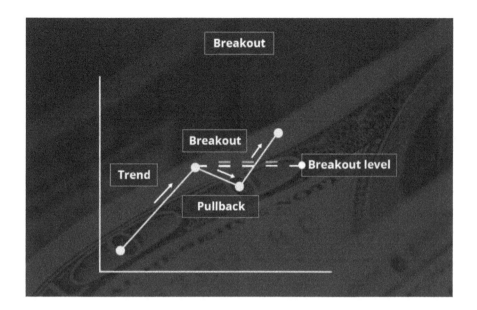

How to find a strong trend

This is the very first step when you are trend trading. Your aim should be to identify a strong trend over a period of time, and you can do this by using a chart to tell whether momentum is behind the market.

If you are going to enter the market, you have to know the direction the markets are trading increasing your chances of having a successful trade. The simplest way to know the direction is to utilize trend lines.

If there is an uptrend you will see that there are rising slopes. This means that you can trade on the bullish or long side of the market until that uptrend ends.

When to enter a trend

Once you know the trend, the next thing is for you to know when to enter the market. Well, in this case, what you need to pay attention to is the pullback. A pullback simply refers to when the market is progressing in a certain direction and then suddenly starts pulling on the opposite direction.

For instance, if you have an asset whose price moves lower while the previous trend was bullish. In other words, you should aim to enter the market at the point where you will be able to trade the market momentum. To do this, you can simply identify the trend first and then look out for that pullback. Then finally, you can aim to trade the breakout, which mirrors momentum agreeing with the long-term trend.

How to determine your pain threshold

Each trade requires risk parameters. Think of your pain threshold as the point at which you need to take prolonged breaks from the market especially following a string of losses.

For instance, you might have incurred a strong of losses four trades in a row. In each trade, you lose 3% of your account balance, amounting to 12% loss of your tradeable equity.

Truth is, this kind of loss will rattle your nerves however good a trader you are. This is a vicious cycle you can avoid by setting suitable limits. So, if your pain threshold is 10%, this simply means that you stand to lose a total of 10% of account balance before making a break. Ensure that you set one that suits you and the amount you are willing to lose.

Trading ranges

Trading ranges occur when a security trades between two consistently high- and lowprice points for a given duration. One thing to note is that each trading range has a support price and resistance, at which traders buy and sell security, respectively.

How to find security in a wide trading range

Here, you simply use the ADX indicators. What you simply need to know here is that the ADX value is below 20, signaling a non-trending market. However, if the value is >30 this indicates a trending market.

It is important to note that the range has to be wide enough to permit for a meaningful profit. For instance, if your stocks trade between $66 and $70, this means that the range is too tight that every profit you make will be beaten up by taxes, commissions among others.

Truth is, there is no rule how to tell when the market is wide enough. However, these are some of the factors to consider when determining the strength of the trade;

Time; the longer the trading range, the higher the chances of it continuing in force.

Touches of support and resistance; the higher the number of times a trade touches support/resistance levels, the more powerful the support/resistance is. Therefore, it is important that you try finding one that has several touches of support and resistance.

Flat ranges; this simply refers to how much a trading range looks like a rectangle. Some trading ranges have support levels that fall and resistance that rises. These regions are suspicious because they do not clearly tell you where true resistance and support lie. In most instances, they create a completely different form of chart. Therefore, the flatter the resistance and support level, the stronger the conviction meaning that the trading ranges are genuine.

How to enter a range

There are a wide range of indicators that a trader can use to enter or exit a trading range. These indicators include; price action and volumes. One of the basic ways to enter a range is be closer to the boundaries.

In other words, you sell when the prices are at the top of the range. On the other hand, you buy when the prices are at the bottom of the range. At the top of the range marks the resistance area for price rise and the bottom marks the support area for price decline.

How to set your exit level

One of the ways to set your exit level is by using relative strength analysis (RSI). This is a momentum-based indicator whose major role is to compare the current strength of an asset and that of a previous period. For most traders, they set their period at 14 meaning that the closing price data is derived from the past 14 periods and then used in calculating the RSI value.

The RSI value oscillates between 0 and 100. This means that if the RSI value drops below 30, it indicates an oversold. If above 70 then it is an indication of an overbought.

If an asset is oversold, then the trade is happening below its true value. This means that there is a high chance of it rebounding to the upside under normal market conditions.

Conversely, if there is an overbought, it indicates that trading is happening at a premium level. Here, the chances are that the correction might happen to the downside.

You can use the RSI value on a macro level to tell if the market conditions are bullish or bearish. If the market is bearish, the typical RSI value would lie between 10 and 60, where 50-60 serves as the resistance level. On the bullish market, the RSI value typically lies between 40 and 90, where 40-50 serves as the support range.

Limitation of technical analysis

Efficient market hypothesis (EMH)

This simply suggests that the markets have information that make it efficient. In other words, the prices and expectations are priced into investments. It also suggests that it is impossible to exceed the average market returns by just reviewing previous data on pricing.

Considering that technical analysis is fully focused on the concept of using past data to anticipate movements in prices likely to happen in the future, EMH is conceptually opposed to technical analysis.

That said, it is important to note that there are at least three versions of EMH where two conclude that technical analysis as well as fundamental analysis are not useful when one is making investment decisions. The other version holds that some fundamental analysis techniques can be used.

Self-fulfilling prophecy

When performing technical analysis, it is quite dangerous to fully rely on the assumption that current prices can be used to predict future prices. Yes, there are instances where they do but not necessarily. This means that replying on charts may not be useful when picking signals about changing trends until they actually happen.

In other words, the chances are that you could miss out on at least 1/3 of your trading currency. With technical analysis, one tends to act on patterns prematurely or panic. When a large number of traders do this, it simply creates a self-fulfilling prophecy. One common argument in this case is that technical analysis is focused on predicting a given outcome based on the pattern of the chart.

This way, you end up ignoring the real reasons for that movement, which are due to key factors. This is one obvious limitation of the technical analysis. Even though certain theories offer a certain level of objectivity, there are studies that do not necessarily yield objective interpretations. This explains the reason why technical analysis is considered an art rather than a science.

Key takeaways

- The main aim of technical analysis is to try and shed light into all the. sentiments the market holds on price trends by focusing on the trends and
  patterns instead of the analyzing attributes of securities.

- Technical analysis makes use of historical price actions when predicting future price actions.

- The main source of technical analysis data is the stock charts.

- Technical analysis is not about making decisions with 100% certainty.

Chapter 2: Perform Intrinsic Value Analysis Like The Oracle Of Omaha Using Fundamental Analysis

Fundamental analysis simply refers to a technique that is used to measure the intrinsic value of a security by evaluating financial factors and related economic factors. Here, the aim is to examine anything that might affect the value of security from macroeconomic factors to microeconomic factors such as effectiveness of management of a company.

The end game here is to come up with a number that an investor can use to compare with the current price of security for them to determine whether it is overvalued or undervalued. Therefore, fundamental analysis is different to technical analysis, which mainly predicts price directions by looking at the historical data in the market about volumes and prices.

Role of Fundamental Analysis For Swing Trading

In spite the fact that earnings are key, truth is that they cannot tell much by themselves. This is mainly because they do not identify the manner in which the market values the stocks by themselves. This means that you need some fundamental analysis tools to build a clear picture of how stocks are valued.

What is important to note is that fundamental analysis is a key component of any successful trading and investment strategy. In other words, all traders need to have a basic knowledge of how fundamental analysis works.

When conducting fundamental analysis, some of the factors that you need to consider include;

- What is the company's revenue?
- Is the revenue growing?
- Are you making profits?
- Is there an increase in the level of dept or payment of debts?
- What are your turnover rates?
- Does the company management take care of its employees?

All these factors play a central role in defining the numeric intrinsic value for security that can be compared to its existing price.

But how does fundamental analysis work?

Fundamental analysis observes a wide range of elements that affect the prices of stocks. Some of these factors are sales, earnings per share among others that we will discuss further in this chapter.

In this case, the analysts simply use the bottom-up or top-down techniques in performing their analysis. In other instances, they use both.

The top-down analysis works in the following ways;

- Analyses the whole market including macroeconomic and global indicators
- Analyses the specific sector like technology
- Analyses the whole industry such as semiconductor manufacturers
- Analyses the specific stock such as Company ABC

On the other hand, the bottom-up analysis simply starts by looking at specific stocks. Here, the main aim of the analyst is to examine the trends, price and market movements, interest rates, financial statements of the company, return on equity (ROE), among other factors. The goal here is to buy or sell stocks that offer a high return on investment (ROI).

Why Does Fundamental Analysis Even Matter?

Just like technical analysis, fundamental analysis focuses on predicting what stocks are valuable and which ones are not. Based on what the proponents of this technique say, fundamental analysis offers a bigger and fuller picture of possible stock market and individual stock movements because so many elements are being investigated.

Perhaps one of the greatest arguments here is that you should use fundamental analysis is by looking at some of the wealthiest most famous proponents like Warren Buffett.

Here are some of the popular fundamental analysis tools;

Price-To-Earnings

This simply refers to a tool that examines the relationship between the prices of stocks and the earnings of the company. It is one of the most popular metrics when performing stock analysis despite the fact that it is far from the one you should consider.

To get the price to earnings value, all you have to do is take the price of a share and divide it by the EPS value of a company.

That is; P/E = price of stock/EPS

For instance, if the price per share in a company is $50 and the EPS is 10, then the price to earnings ratio will be $50/10 = 5.

What does that even mean? Well, the P/E value gives you an idea of what the market is likely to pay for the earnings of the company. In other words, if the P/E value is high, it indicates that there is a high chance the market will fork over.

Other investors will tell you that the P/E value tells you when stocks are overpriced. While that might be the case in some instances, it could also be indicative of a market that has high hopes for the future of its stocks hence bidding up the prices.

Conversely, having a low P/E may indicate a vote of no confidence by the market. In other words, there is a sleeper known as value stocks the market has chosen to overlook before the rest discover its true worth.

But what is the right P/E value? Well, the answer here depends on whether you are willing to pay for the earnings. This means that, if you are highly willing -indicating your trust in the company- the higher the right P/E for that specific stock when making decisions.

That said, there are investors who will not see the value in this and will consider the right P/E as wrong. Whatever the case, if you are using the P/E value, it is important that you know how to turn it into a potential successful investment.

Earnings-Per-Share

If you want to compare stocks between a wide range of publicly held companies, it is critical that you learn how to calculate their earnings per share (EPS). You will notice that the greatest challenge is doing a comparison of "apples to apples" between companies that are not dissimilar. However, with the use of EPS, you can do a meaningful comparison that will go a long way in helping you make informed choices.

When you compare the price of two stocks, that will tell you nothing. In the same way, when you compare the earnings of one company and that of another, there is no meaning in that. This is mainly because when you use the raw numbers, you are choosing to ignore the fact that these two companies have varied number of outstanding shares among several other differences.

However, it is more sensible to use EPS as a comparison tool. For instance, if you have company A and B with a net income of $150. Company A has 15 stocks outstanding while B has 50 outstanding. This means that, if you were to own company A, you have a high chance of getting higher rewards especially if the company pays dividends since the same earnings are spread between 15 shareholders rather than 50.

How do you determine earnings per sale?

Here, you simply take the net earnings of your target company and divide that by the firm's outstanding shares.

EPS = Net earnings/outstanding shares

Let us consider the example we just talked about earlier of Company A and B. Here, the EPS value of company A would be ($150/15=10). On the other hand, company B would have an EPS value of ($150/50=3).

In such a case, you should proceed to buy company A with an EPS of 10, right? Well, the best thing is to hold off on using the EPS value alone in decision making. The thing is, EPS plays a central role when comparing between two companies given that they are in the same industry. However, it will not tell you whether their stocks are good to buy and what the market's perception is about them.

There are three types of EPS numbers; trailing EPS, current EPS and forward EPS.

Trailing EPS simply refer to the previous year's numbers and the actual EPS. Current EPS is the current year's numbers that are still projections. Finally, forward EPS refer to future numbers that are obviously projections.

When you know these forms of EPS numbers, you will be in a better position to compare the stocks. However, you will still require additional information to determine whether any one of them is worth investing in.

Return-On-Equity

This is a measure of how efficient a company utilizes its assets in producing earnings. Therefore, when you understand this value, you are in a better position to evaluate stocks.

To calculate the ROE, you simply divide the net income by the book value. If the ROE value lies between 13-15%, this indicates that the company is healthy. Just like all other metrics, comparing companies that are within the same industry will help you get a clear picture of what is happening.

That said, the ROE does not come without flaws that might actually blur the picture. This means that you should not rely on the ROE alone when making an investment decision.

For instance, you might get a company with a large debt and tries to raise funds by borrowing rather than issuing stocks. This way, its book value reduces. When the book value is low, it indicates that you have to divide it by a smaller number so that the ROE value is high artificially.

The book value can also be reduced by taking such factors as stocks buy-backs, write-downs, and other accounting sleights off the hand. This only raises the ROE value without necessarily improving profits.

It is also important that you analyze the ROE over a duration of 5 years instead of one year. This way, you will be able to average out any numbers that are abnormal. Considering the fact that you have to look at the whole picture, ROE will help you identify the companies with competitive advantage.

Projected Earnings Growth

This simply translates to price/earnings to growth ratio. To calculate PEG value, you take the price to earnings ratio and then divide it by the projected growth in earnings. It's based on annual earnings growth and relies on predictions that might not really be accurate all the time. In other words, projections naturally are not an exact science.

When you look at the market, you will realize that the major concern here is the future and not preset. In that case, there is need to look for ways that will project out and forward. To do this, the PEG ratio plays a key role in helping you calculate the future earnings growth. It puts into account the rate of projected earnings growth to the P/E.

PEG = P/E/ projected growth in earnings

Just like all other ratios, PEG shows relationships. In this instance, if the PEG number is lower, this indicates that you will pay less for every unit of future earnings growth. A stock with a high P/E value and a projected earnings growth that is high can also be considered a good value.

On the contrary, when the P/E stock value is low and there is no projected earnings growth, it may seem like a value that will not work out. For instance, if the P/E for a stock is 8 and the PEG is 8, this might actually be a very expensive investment to make.

Price-To-Book Ratio

When you think of some of the greatest stock market investors in the world, the first thing that comes to mind is the likes of Benjamin Graham and Warren Buffett among others. These are some of the proponents of value investing. Price to book ratio is the only fundamental analysis metrics that is associated with value.

While it may be impossible to attain Warren Buffet's wealth, you can choose to be a member on a quiet group that invests in the long-term game.

To define this ration, you can say that it is a financial ratio that plays a central role when comparing the current market price of a company and its book value. It is also referred to as the market-to-book ratio.

The idea behind long-term value investing is to identify the market sleeper other investors passed and then hold on to them as companies go about their business without really drawing attention from the market. Then without any warning, the sleeper stocks hit the screens of those that discover and bid them up. Meanwhile, as a value investor, you get to walk away with a hefty profit that sometimes make you wealthy.

Ways to calculate the P/B ratio

If you choose to calculate the ratio using the first method, then you simply extract the company's total book value from the balance sheets. However, if you use the per share value method, then you have to ensure that you divide the current share price of the company by the book value per share. In other words, you are calculating it by dividing by the number of shares outstanding.

As we have mentioned earlier, when comparing companies ensure that they are within the same industry. However, if there is variation in the industry, you will notice that those that require more infrastructure trade a much lower P/B ratio.

P/B ratios are mostly used when comparing banks mainly because their assets and liabilities are valued at market value. When the P/B ratio is high, this indicates that investors expect that company management will create more value from a particular set of assets. However, you cannot use the P/B ratio to get information on the company's ability to generate profits for its shareholders.

Dept-In-Equity (D/E) Ratio

The main aim of this metric is to compare the total liabilities of a company to the equity of its shareholders so that you are better placed to evaluate how much leverage a company uses. To obtain this value, you divide the total liabilities of a company by the shareholder's equity. You can get these values from the financial statements of a company.

The D/E ratio tells you more about the company's financial leverage. In other words, it measures the extent to which a company finances its operations by way of debt versus its own funds. Particularly, it reflects the shareholder equity's ability to cover outstanding debts in case the business downturns.

D/E ratio = Total liabilities /Total shareholder's equity

All information can be obtained from the balance sheet as earlier mentioned. What you need to note is that the balance sheet requires total shareholders' equity to be equal to the assets minus liabilities;

Assets = Liabilities + shareholder equity

What is interesting is that these balance sheet categories may not really contain individual accounts that would otherwise be classified as debt or equity in a traditional sense of things. Considering the fact that the ratio can be distorted by intangible assets, retained earnings and losses, as well as pension plan adjustments, there is need for a more comprehensive research to determine the company's true leverage.

Based on the ambiguity seen in some accounts' primary balance sheet, most investors will modify the D/E ratio so that it is more useful and easier to use when comparing between varied stocks. You can also improve the analysis of the D/E ratio by including growth expectations, profit performance and leverage ratios.

The bottom line is if the leverage ratio is high, it implies that the company has a higher risk to shareholders. That said, the D/E ratio is quite complex to compare across industry groups where there is ideal variation in debt.

Finally, investors often modify the D/E ratio such that it focuses on the long-term debt alone because the risk associated with long-term liabilities is different compared to short-term debts and payables.

Total Revenue

In as much as Earnings per share can offer the investor a clear sense of how well a company's business model is working, the total revenue is a brilliant indicator that tells us how much business a certain company is dealing with.

When you see a positive trend in revenue, this implies that the business is expanding/growing. For instance, if you look at large companies like Amazon.com and Netflix among others. They register a high growth but they may go for so many years without necessarily generative positive EPS. This is mainly because these kinds of companies invest their profits in growing the business. Conversely, a company that is struggling like Macy's may generate consistent amount of profits despite its revenue being down by 11% over the past 5 years.

Key takeaways

- The aim of Fundamental Analysis is to examine anything that might affect the value of security from macroeconomic factors to microeconomic factors such as effectiveness of management of a company.

- The analysts simply use the bottom-up or top-down techniques in performing their analysis.

- When you compare the price of two stocks, that will tell you nothing. In the same way, when you compare the earnings of one company and that of another, there is no meaning in that.

- When you see a positive trend in revenue, this implies that the business is expanding/growing.

- Fundamental analysis is the opposite of technical analysis, which mainly predicts price directions by looking at the historical data in the market about volumes and prices.

Chapter 3: Proven Risk Management Techniques To Stay Profitable

One thing that will determine whether you will be a successful trader/investor is how well you manage risks. When investing, some of the questions that you need to ask yourself are;

Is the security liquid? I

s that security a penny stock?

Are you ready to limit your losses at the level of individual stocks?

The main reason why you are doing this is to ensure that you have set precautionary measures based on the percentage of stake you are willing to lose say ~0.25% - 2% of your total assets. Additionally, you can choose to set the risk level as a direct percentage of assets and that percentage should not exceed 10% of your overall portfolio.

Risk Assessment Before Buying

Beta assessment

When you think of beta assessment, this is simply a measure of how volatile stocks are in the market. The market is said to have a beta of 1.0. Here, individual stocks are ranked based on how much they deviate from the market. If the stock swings more than the market over time, then it is said to have a beta>1. Conversely, the stock moves less than the market then its beta value is <1.

This simply means that the higher the beta value, the riskier the stocks. That said, these kinds of stocks often offer higher returns as opposed to those with a lower beta and are associated with lower risk levels and returns.

Conducting beta assessment goes a long way in telling us more about the capital asset pricing model that is otherwise used in calculating equity costs. One thing that you need to remember is that the capital cost goes a long way in helping one arrive at the existing value of a company's future cash flows. All things constant, the higher the beta of a company, the higher the capital cost discount rate.

In other words, the present value of the company is lower meaning that the beta assessment can actually impact the share valuation of a company. To calculate the beta, you use the regression analysis. Just to reiterate, beta represents the tendency of a company's security returns to respond to market swings.

Some of the advantage of conducting a beta assessment of a company is the fact that it can tell you a lot about price variability of stocks, which is key in assessing risk. Are you thinking of risk as the possibility of your stocks losing value? Well, then beta is your proxy for that risk.

Well this makes a lot of sense. Just try to think back to an early stage technology stock that had a price fluctuating more than the market. What is the first thing that comes to mind? Definitely that the stocks are riskier than a utility stock with a low beta value.

The good thing with conducting a beta assessment is the fact that it offers a clear and more quantifiable measure that is quite easy to work with. While there may be variations in beta based on a wide range of factors like market index and the time period of measurement, it is fairly straightforward when calculating the costs of equity utilized in valuation, which reveals future cash flows.

That said, beta assessment is not without its disadvantages. For instance, if you are investing in stocks, beta does not consider new information. Let is consider a utility company X with defensive stocks having a low beta. As it joined the merchant energy business and assumed high levels of debt, the historic beta of Company X stopped considering the substantial risk the company took on. Similarly, so many technology stocks in the company are new in the market meaning that they have insufficient price history when establishing a reliable beta.

Additionally, movements of prices are one of the poorest predictors of the future. Think of beta assessment as a rear-view mirror that only tells you very little of what is actually ahead. Also, considering a beta measure on just a single stock has a tendency of flipping around over time, making it quite unreliable. Therefore, if you are looking to purchase and sell stocks within a short duration, then beta is a good risk metric. However, if you are looking to invest long-term, this may not be the best way to go.

Assessing risk?

Well, when you think of risk, you are simply talking about the possibility of suffering a loss, right? When an investor considers a risk, what is going through their mind is the possibility of the stocks they buy decreasing in value. The problem is, bet as a proxy for risk does not differentiate between an upside and downside as far as price movements in the market.

For many investors, having a downside movement is a risk while an upside movement is an opportunity worth leveraging. However, does it tell the investors what the difference is? Certainly not! This is why it does not make a lot of sense. "Well, it may be all right in practice, but it will never work in theory."

- Warren Buffet

The truth is, most value investors scorn the idea of using beta in risk assessment. This is mainly because it implies that stocks have had a sharp fall in value making it riskier than it was before. You may argue that a company has a lower-risk investment if their value falls. The truth is, investors can still get the same stocks at a lower price despite the fact that the stock's beta increased after its fall. In other words, beta will tell you nothing about the price paid for the stocks with regard to its future cash flows.

The bottom line is, it is critical to differentiate between short-term risks and long-term risks, where beta and price volatility is useful and risk factors are more telling, respectively. Yes, high betas may imply price volatility in the near term but the truth is that they do not always have to rule out long-term opportunities.

Limiting losses

It is true that no one wants to lose their money when playing in the market. This is why you have to set your position in a security, hence the stop-loss orders. However, it is quite challenging for most investors to determine where to set their threshold levels. This is because, if they set them up too high, then they risk incurring big losses in case the market makes a move in the opposite direction. It is critical that you set the position close enough to make your exit strategy quick and easy.

The main aim of a stop loss order is to sell securities when they reach a set price. Determining where to place your stop-loss often depends on what your risk threshold is. In other words, the price you choose should be central in limiting losses.

Assessing your threshold

There are so many methods used in limiting losses such as the percentage method, which limits loses at a certain percentage. In the support method, as an investor, your role is to determine the most recent level of stocks and then setting your stop-loss just below it. on the other hand, the moving average method aims at placing the stop-loss limit right below a long-term moving average price.

One of the most common levels that is acceptable for limiting losses is at 2% of the equity in your trading account. The capital you have in your trading account is often referred to as your risk capital, which you use each day to garner profits.

Assessing your threshold should be done even before you enter the trade. In other words, when you are deciding on how much of a certain trading instrument you would like to buy, it would be important that you calculate how much losses you are likely to sustain on the trade without having to breach your 2% rule.

In the same way, you would set your position within a maximum of 2% loss of your total equity. Your stop can be anything between 0 and 2% total loss. This means that a higher risk level is acceptable if an individual trade calls for it.

If you ask every trader, they will have a different opinion of the 2% rule. There are those who think that a 2% risk limit is way too small and that it has a tendency of stifling their ability to take part in riskier trading decisions with a bigger chunk of their trading account.

On the other hand, most professionals will tell you that 2% is ridiculously high and their preference would be to limit their losses to 0.25-0.5% of their portfolios. Well, the pros would naturally incur more risk than those whose accounts are smaller, considering 2% loss on a large portfolio can have a huge impact on their stakes. Irrespective of your capital size, it is critical that you exercise conservatism instead of being aggressive when devising your trading strategy.

Assessing your position size

Determining how big or small your position is should never be a decision you make randomly. The position size is often calibrated for the trade risk as well as personal risk limit. In other words, your position size can make or break you. If you make one big move in the market, there is a chance that your entire account can be wiped down in blink of an eye.

It is critical that you do not allow this happen to you. So, what is this position size anyway? Well, this simply refers to the size of a position within a given portfolio. In other words, it is the dollar amount an investor is willing to trade. Most investors use position sizing when determining the number if security units they can buy to control risk while still maximizing profits.

To assess your position size, you have to go through three steps;

Step 1: determine account risk

It is critical that you determine the risk om your account. This is typically expressed as a percentage of your capital. As mentioned above, it is a rule of thumb to not risk more than 2% of your total investment capital per trade.

For instance, if you have $20,000 capital in your account and decide to set the risk at 2%, it means that you cannot risk more than $400/trade. Even if you lose 10 trades consecutively, you will have lost only 20% of your investment capital.

Step 2: determine trade risk

Once you know the risk of your account, then you have to determine where to set your stop-loss threshold for each trade. If you are trading stocks, the trade risk simply means the distance between the stop-loss price and the entry price.

For instance, if you intend to buy Amazon.com at $150 and the stop-loss order is set at $130, then the trade risk is the difference, which is $20/share.

Step 3: determine the proper position size

At this point, you now know you can risk $400/trade and $20/share. Therefore, to calculate the right position size, you will need to divide the account risk by the trade risk. In this case, it will be $400/$20 which is 20. This means that you can only buy 20 shares in each trade.

Build Your Low-Risk Portfolio

The most important question you need to ask is whether your portfolio is diversified. It is important that your position is spread across a wide range of market capitalizations such as large cap, mid cap, and small cap; across various sectors, and asset classes.

The 7%-rule

Think about limiting your portfolio losses to <7%. Ensure that you cover all your bases to confirm that. Realize that each security on your portfolio possess a risk that is equal to the difference between the stop loss level and the existing price. The difference on individual security level is often tight when it is set at 0.5% and the sum of this difference should not exceed 7% of the total value of your portfolio. The stop loss levels represent profits while barring a gap on prices.

Diversification in Swing Trading

This simply refers to a technique that is aimed at lowering risks by simply allocating investments among a wide range of financial instruments such as different industries. The main aim here is maximize returns by simply investing in many areas that would have different reactions to a similar event.

Despite the fact that diversification does not guarantee against loss, it serves as a key component in reaching long-range financial goals while minimizing risk potential.

There are two major types of risks that investors confront when investing; undiversifiable and diversifiable.

Undiversifiable risks are also referred to as market risks or systematic risks. This is the kind of risk that is often associated with every company with the common causes being war, interest rates, exchange rates, political instability, and inflation rate among others.

These risks are not really specific to a company and cannot be eliminated or reduced by diversification. It is just that risk that an investor has no option but to accept. One thing you need to note about systematic risks is that it affects the market in its entirety and not just a single investment vehicle.

Conversely, diversifiable risks are also referred to as unsystematic risks, and are often very specific to the company, economy, market or country in question. Unlike the former, diversifiable risks can be addressed by diversification. Some of the most common sources of these risks include financial risks and business risks. Hence, the aim here is to invest in a wide range of assets so that they are not affected the same way by the prevailing market events.

So, why should you diversify when swing trading?

Consider that you have a portfolio of airline stocks alone. If the airline pilots announced that they are going on strike indefinitely and all flights are cancelled as a result, the share prices will drop for the airline stocks. What does that mean for your portfolio?

There will be a noticeable decline in value as well, right?

The truth is, if you counterbalanced the airline stocks with say railway stocks, this means that only a portion of your portfolio will be affected. As a matter of fact, there is a really good chance that the prices of railway stock would increase. This is because those who would use air transport will seek alternative form of transportation.

Good thing is, you can diversify further considering that there are so many risks affecting air and rail. Understand that any event that happens and reduces any form of travel will ultimately hurt both companies. According to statistics, air and rail stocks are strongly correlated.

When you diversify your portfolio, you will simply be ensuring that you are not putting all your eggs in one basket. Therefore, it is important that you diversify across the board, not just different companies but also different industries. When your stocks are uncorrelated, the better for you.

Additionally, it is critical to diversify among a varied class of assets. Such assets as stocks and bonds are likely to react in different ways to adverse events. However, if you have a combination of asset classes, the sensitivity to the market swings will be significantly reduced.

Generally, you have to note that equity markets and bonds often move in opposite directions. This means that if you have a diversified portfolio across the two areas, positive results in one will help offset negative outcomes in another.

The other thing is the aspect of location. Diversification also means looking for investment opportunities beyond your geographical location. This is mainly because if there is volatility in the U.S that does not necessarily mean that the stock and bonds in Europe will be affected. Therefore, investing in that part of the world promises to minimize and offset risks associated with investing at home.

But is diversification in swing trading always a good thing? Well, the truth is that there are a number of disadvantages associated with diversification. One thing is for sure, it is hard to manage a diverse portfolio. This is especially the case when you have to manage a various investments and holdings.

Secondly, your bottom line might suffer a dent. Well, the truth is that not all investment vehicles have the same cost. This means that buying and selling may be quite expensive considering the transaction fees and brokerage charges among other costs. Since high risk is associated with high returns, there is a chance that you will limit what you finally come out with.

There are several other forms of diversifications that several synthetic investment products have created to take care of the risk tolerance levels of the investor. Truth is, these products may be complicated and not meant to be created by small investors. If you have less investment experience and have no financial backing to enter into such hedging activities, the most popular way you can diversify is through bonds.

In spite the best analysis of a company along with its financial statements, this still does not guarantee you won't lose your investment. In other words, diversifying will not prevent losses from occurring. However, this can lower the impact of bad information and fraud on your portfolio.

So, you may then ask, "how many stocks should I have?" Well, obviously having 10 stocks is better than having two. But, there will come a time when adding stocks to your portfolio will not make any difference. There are heated debates over how many stocks one should have to lower risks while still enjoying high returns. Most conventional view says that an investor can attain optimal diversification with between 15-20 stocks, provided they are spread across a wide range of industries.

The bottom line here is, diversification plays a significant role in helping you as an investor to manage your risks while lowering the volatility of price movements of assets. What you need to bear in mind is that there is no right or wrong way to diversify your portfolio because risks can never be eliminated entirely.

However, you can lower the risk that is associated with individual stocks. Truth is that the general market risks affects almost all stocks hence the need to diversify across asset classes. The secret here is to strike a balance by finding a medium between returns and risks so that you achieve your financial goals and still have a good night sleep!

Exit At Minimal Risk

Exiting profitable trades

One of the best ways to exit the market at minimal risks is exiting trades that are profitable. In other words, you raise your stop such that you break even as soon as a new trade makes a profit. The good thing with this is that it builds on your confidence considering that you now have a free trade.

After which, you can sit back and allow it to run until prices hit about 75% of the distance between reward targets and risks. At this point, you now have an option to exit the market all at once or bit by bit. It is this kind of decision that tracks the position size and the strategy you choose to employ.

For instance, it does not make any sense to break a small trade into simpler parts. It is more effective if you seek an opportune moment to apply the stop-at-reward strategy.

If you have a large position, this could benefit from a tiered exit strategy. In other words, you exit a third of the trade at 75% of the distance between return targets and risks. Then the second third, you exit at the target. Then finally, you place a trailing stop just after the third piece soon as it exceeds the target, such that you use it as a rock-bottom exit if things turn against your plans.

Over time, you will notice that this third piece is your lifesaver by generating substantial returns. Eventually, you will need to make an exception to the tiered strategy. This is because, there are times when the market hands out gifts and it is your responsibility to pick that low-hanging fruit. This way, when a new shock triggers a significant gap your way, you immediately exit the whole position without any regrets.

Exit based on stop-loss level

Stops often get you out whenever there is a security violation of the technical reasons that made you take the trade in the first place. Well, if you are a trader who knows that you place stops based on arbitrary values, this can be very confusing. This is mainly because these placements do not make much sense when they are tuned to the specific instrument features and volatility.

Instead, you simply use violations of such technical features as trendlines, moving averages, round numbers to establish a natural stop loss price.

Let us consider a company stock that rips high when there is a steady uptrend. It simply stalls >$20 before pulling back to a 3-month trendline. The next bounce goes back to high level, which encourages traders to join the long position as they anticipate a breakout. Here, commonsense tells you that the trendline proofs this wrong, calling for an immediate exit. Additionally, the 20-day simple moving average aligns with the trendline causing an increase in the odds that a violation will attract selling pressure.

In effective stop placements, there is need for an additional step especially in the modern markets. Today, algorithms target common stop loss levels causing a shake out of retail players, before it jumps back across resistance and support. This means that the stops have to be placed away from the numbers that tell you that you are wrong and need to exit.

Finding the perfect price to avoid these stop runs is something that is more art than it is a science. A general rule of thumb is that an additional 10-15 cents should function in a trade that has low volatility. However, a momentum play will need an additional 50-75 cents. Therefore, if you are watching in real-time, you have more options because you can exit at the original risk target and then reenter if the prices go back across the contested levels.

Exist based on passage of time

It is important to establish your risk targets and rewards prior to entering trades. It is critical that you look at the chart to know when the next resistance level is likely to happen within your holding period. This marks the reward target. Then the next thing is for you to find the price where you will be proven wrong in case the security turns south and hits it. This is your risk target.

From here, you can now calculate your reward/risk ratio to find at least a 2:1 in your favor. If you get anything less than that, then it is advisable to skip the trade and move on to find a better opportunity. Focus the trade management on two key exit prices.

Consider a situation where things are working in your favor and the advancing price is moving towards your reward target. Here, the price rate of change come in to play because the sooner you get to the magic number, the more flexibility you attain when selecting the best time to exit.

The first option for you is to take a blind exit at the price and then move on to the next trade with a smile on your face. When the price is trending strongly in your favor, the best thing to do is to allow it to exceed the reward target before you place a protective stop at that point as you try to add more gains. After that, you need to look at the next evident barrier so that you stay put ensuring that it is not in violation of your holding period.

Slow advances are quite tricky to trade because several securities will approach but not get to the reward target. This is something that needs a profit protection strategy that gets into action soon as the price traverses 75% of the distance between reward target and risk. It is critical that at this point, you place a trailing stop that will offer protection to your profits.

Alternatively, if you are trading real-time, you simply keep one of your fingers on the exit button as you keep an eye on the ticker. The secret is to ensure that you stay put until the price action gives you reason beyond doubt to exit.

Key takeaways

- Being a successful trader/investor is about how well you manage risks.

- High betas may imply price volatility in the near term, but the truth is that they do not always rule out long-term opportunities.

- Determining where to place your stop-loss often depends on what your risk threshold is.

- If you make one big move in the market, there is a chance that your entire account can be wiped down in blink of an eye.

- Diversification helps investors manage their risks while lowering the volatility of price movements of assets.

- Risk can be both undiversifiable or systemic, and diversifiable or un-systemic.

- Investors tend to think of balancing a diversified portfolio as a complex and costly thing, and it may come with lower rewards because the risk is mitigated.

Chapter 4: Winning Entry And Exit Strategies

Monitoring Of The Main Order Types

Market orders

One thing to note about market orders is that they buy and sell at the current price, irrespective of what the price is. The market orders often get filled in an active market but not necessarily in the price the trader intended.

For instance, you may place a market order when the best price is 1.1954 but then other orders get filled first and your order might get filled at 1.1955 instead.

Note that market orders get used when you need yours to be processed but are willing to getting a slightly different price from what you wanted. If you are making a purchase, chances are that your market order will get filled at the asking price. This is mainly because that price is what someone else is willing to sell for.

On the other hand, if you are selling, there is a chance that your market order might get filled at the bid price. This is because that might just be the price someone else is willing to purchase at.

Limit orders

These simply refer to orders used when buying or selling an asset at a particular price or better. Unlike the market orders, limit orders may or may not get filled and this depends on the manner in which the market is moving. However, if the limit orders get filled, it always will be at the chosen price, or even better.

For instance, if you placed a limit order with a price of $40.50, then the order would get filled at $40.50, or even better. In this situation, the better price would be $50.50, in case it got filled at all.

When you want to get a suitable price and are willing to get your order not filled at all, then the limit orders are the way to go. Note that the order only gets filled if the person selling is willing to sell to you if you are selling at $40.50, or below.

If you intend to sell at $40.50, or even better, this means that you would prefer to use a sell limit order. This order will only be executed if another person is willing to buy from you at $40.50, or more.

Stop orders

These ones are quite similar to market orders in the sense that they are orders in which you can buy and sell assets at the best prices available. However, these orders are only processed if the market reaches a particular price.

For instance, if the existing asset price is 1.2444, you might place a buy stop order at 1.2476. this means that if the market trades at 1.2476 or more, your stop order would be processed as a market order and get filled at the current best price.

The processing of stop orders is quite similar to that of market orders. This means that once you reach the stop or trigger price, the orders will always get filled.
However, this is not necessarily at the price the trader intended in the first place.

Truth is, stop orders often trigger the market trades at or beyond the stop price.

For a buy order, it is critical that the stop price is above the existing price. For a sell order, the stop price has to be below the existing price. You can use a stop order to enter the trade and also to exit the trade as a stop loss.

For instance, if you buy stocks at $40.50 you may place a sell stop at say $40.25. This means that if the price reaches $40.25 and below, the sell order gets executed. This is what will get you out of position at $40.25 or below, hence limiting the loss on that position.

However, if you are short at $40.50, you may choose to place a buy stop at $40.75 in order to limit losses. If the price reaches $40.75 and more, the buy stop gets executed and closes the trade at $40.75 or more.

Stop limit orders

It is common for traders to combine both a stop and a limit order for the sake of finetuning the price they get. To open a trade, you could place a stop limit at $40.75. Assuming the stocks are currently trading at $40.50, when the price reaches $40.75 there will be execution of the stop limit order. However, this is only the case if the order is executed at $40.75, or below.

This goes a long way in initiating a short position. Take an instance where the current market price is 30.50 and the trader wants to go short if the price drops to $30.30, then they can set the sell stop at this point. Therefore, once the price reaches $30.30, the order gets executed but only if the order gets to this price target or above. That said, stop orders often remain pending until someone is willing to trade at the stop limit order price, or even better.

Entry And Exit Strategies For Part-Time Traders

There is a big difference between full-time and part-time trading. Part-time trading can be very tricky because trading does not always follow the usual trajectory.

One thing that is important to note is that trading is about quality and not quantity. In other words, if you do not get suitable trades, you can forgo trading those days even if it takes weeks at the same time.

However, just because trades are not suitable does not necessarily mean that you should not work. It is important that you keep educating yourself on how to interpret the watchlist and be ready for when opportunities present themselves.

Entering the fray

When you are trading part-time, your entry weapon is a limit order. However, if you have access to algo trading types, you can use an algo with an attached limit order. This means that, when a buy signal presents itself on a certain day, what you need to do is review how prices are behaving during the day so that you can determine the best point to place a reasonable buy order.

It is good to be choosy. However, if your limit order is not filled there is no big deal. Remember that there are plenty of fish in the sea and you only need to wait the next time to cast your net again.

When you don't chase after the security so desperately, you can enter the trade on your terms soon as prices are favorable to you.

The last thing you want is trading the open market. It is chaotic when the emerging news after the market closed the day before is mirrored in the opening prices. Truth is, there can be major swings, both negative and positive.

The other point to note is to never enter a market order when the market is closed. This is because such a market order will be executed at the next day's opening prices, irrespective of what the price is. Truth is, movements are often fierce at the opening and entering market orders the previous day will be too much uncertainty of where the prices are likely to be executed.

What if you want to buy shares at the closing price the day before? The truth is that the market order will be executed here significantly above or below the price based on the prevailing conditions in the market. Just bear in mind the ol' Wall Street saying;
"Amateurs trade the open while professionals trade the close."

Exiting to cut losses or make a profit

When you buy stocks, the first thing that you need to do is set an initial stop loss point. This is important in ensuring that your capital is protected in case the stocks go against you. there are two major kinds that you can use in your exit strategy to cut losses or make profits. These are;

Physical stop loss order: This refers to an order to sell or buy (only if you are short) that you place with a broker

Mental stop: this simply refers to you clicking on the sell button or the buy button just so that you can exit the trade.

From a technical point of view, it really does not matter what type of stop loss order you choose to use. However, it is critical that before getting into any trade, you develop a plan that will help you determine when to exit the trade whenever things don't work out in your favor.

Are you a disciplined trader that always follows their plan through? If that's the case, then you are safe. This is because, when trading, it is always important to exit the trade based on your already predetermined plan. But where is that stop going to be?

Well, your stop should be sensible and out of the noise of current activities in sticks happening in the market.

But why use a stop clock? The truth is, when you buy stocks, you anticipate that they go in your favor. However, if things go south, you don't have to keep waiting for things to start moving in the desired direction. What you need to do is sell you shares and proceed to something else. The last thing you want is having all your capital tied up on a stock that is trading sideways. Treat your stocks like employees, if they are not performing, then fire them.

The second strategy is for you to use price alerts. If the prices cross at this level, you will want to be informed so that you can effectively manage your trades. The main aim here is to reduce the chart time so that you don't spend all your time doubting your original trade ideas.

With price alerts, you think way ahead on the level you would want to act. The what if scenarios will help you determine how you intend to manage your trades beforehand so that you can see where to exit and at what point your take profits will likely be. If you also want to scale in and out of positions, price alerts are a great option. All you have to do is set the alerts at suitable price levels and you are good to go!

Finally, you need to determine the right profit levels. According to statistics, it is safe to say that profit levels give better results if they are supported by market data. This simply means that for every trade, you need to know what the chart pattern, volatility data, and market structure looks like. This will help you know whether they support price movements in what direction.

Avoid setting take profit levels at random prices.

When you use this approach, you are better positioned to accomplish a number of things. First, considering that your take profits is not an arbitrary value, there is a high chance that the price moves to this level just to test it.

Second, it is important that you determine whether your Risk: Reward ratio is worth it depending on the levels that is directed by the data and structure of the market, which is more sensible.

So, how do I know my take profit level?

First, you need to look at the pair to trade and start looking for resistance and support on the chart. Look for regions of the chart where prices have seen bigger activities in the past. Well, this does not necessarily mean that prices will move to those levels. However, there is a tendency of prices retesting existing support and resistance levels as shown in the figure below;

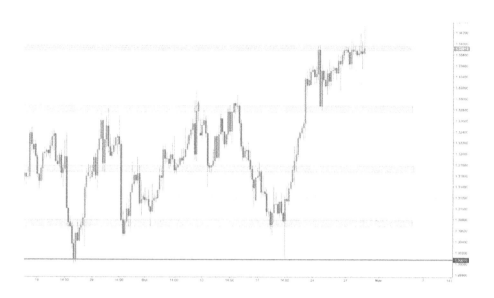

In the case of a buy order, it is critical that you place your take profit levels a number of pips below the resistance. Conversely, when using a sell order, simply place the take profit level a number above the support. This accounts for everything like spread and is much safer than setting your stop loss on the actual level.

One thing you need to look for when determining the take profit levels is the trend lines, moving averages, and spikes in price activity. However, in my experience, I have found that prices often adhere to horizontal levels.

Entry And Exit Strategies For Full-Time Traders

Benefit from intraday charting to time entry and exit

Did you know that day traders are traders that execute intraday strategies so that they can profit off of changes in prices for a set of assets? When you select the sweetest stock in the market, the next thing is for you to profit from them and the best thing is to rely on suitable strategies.

There are so many intraday strategies available in the market. However, sticking to the guidelines and identifying intraday trading signals can be challenging. So, when do you know when to benefit from intraday charting to time entry and exit?

Trade only with the current intraday trend

One thing you need to note is that the market often moves in waves. This means that it is the responsibility of the trader to ride the waves. When there is an uptrend, your aim should be to take long positions. On the other hand, if there is a downtrend, it is important that you aim at taking short positions.

The thing with intraday trends is that they do not continue indefinitely. When you have a dominant trend shift, then it is advisable to trade a new trend. But how can you isolate trends?

Well, this is the difficult part. With trendlines, you get an idea of where a useful entry and stop-loss strategy is. When you draw in more trendlines, you gain access to more signals that offer greater insight into the changes in the market dynamics.

Trade strong stocks in the uptrend and weak ones in the downtrend

If you are looking for stocks for intraday trading, the most beneficial thing is to look for ETFs or equities that possess at least a moderate to high correlation with the S&P 500 as well as the Nasdaq indices. After which, you isolate the stocks that are strong from those that are relatively weak based on the index.

This way, you create an opportunity for the day trader considering that strong stocks move up at least by 2% when the indices move a percent. Truth is, fast moving stocks offer more opportunity.

Reversion-to-the-mean trading

This is a theory that explains how extreme events are often followed by normal ones. In other words, there is a tendency for things to even out with time. For instance, you might see a soccer team score unusual goals in a match and in the coming matches, there is a chance that they will score closer to their average.

How do you apply this strategy?

The best way is to seek out extreme events and then bet that things revert to anything closer to the average. However, the only challenge is the fact that the financial market is not distributed normally. There is a long tail and there is a chance that extreme events cluster together. In turn, the feedback loops may escalate and create momentum which affects reversion.

When the stocks drop 10% on a certain day, chances are that they will drop even further the following day. Despite that, traders can use mean reversion to find an edge and then build their trading strategies around it.

When there is a simple mean reversion, you could buy stocks after a drastic drop in prices with the hope that the stocks will rebound to a normal level. There are so many ways in which mean reversion is applied;

- With technical indicators
- With Financial Information
- With Economic Indicators
- With Sentiment Indicators

Heikin-ashi technique

This is a technique that plays a central role in averaging price data with the aim of creating Japanese candlesticks that aim at filtering out all market noise. This technique uses a modified formula that is based on two-period averages based, which give the chart a smoother appearance. This makes it seamless to spot trends and reversals while obscuring gaps and price data.

What does Heikin-Ashi say? Well, this is often used by traders to identify a trend easily. When there is an uptrend, hollow white/green candles without lower shadows are evident on the chart. On the other hand, a downtrend is seen when there is a filled black/red candle without upper shadows.

Considering that the Heikin-Ashi technique smooths the price information over a span of two periods, it renders the trends, reversal points, and price patterns quite easy to spot. The thing with the Heikin-Ashi charts is that they typically have more consecutive colored candles that play an important role in helping traders identify past price movements with ease.

They also help in lowering occurrence of false trading signals especially in sideways and choppy markets, which helps one avoid placing trades at these times. For instance, instead of getting two false reversal candles before the beginning of a trend, using Heikin-Ashi technique increases the likelihood of getting a valid signal.

Limitations of the Heikin-Ashi technique

- Considering that this technique uses two periods, it often takes longer for it to develop making it quite unresponsive for day traders who would like to leverage fast movements in prices.
- The averaged data in this case also obscures important information on prices. In other words, the actual daily closing price is not seen on the Heikin-Ashi chart.

Fibonacci analysis

This is one of the most popular tools for technical traders. This is mainly because the Fibonacci retracement is created by simply taking two extreme points on a stock chart and then dividing the distance by the ratios of say 23.6%, 38.2%, 50%, 61.8%, and 100%.

Once the levels are known, the horizontal lines are then drawn and used in determining what resistance and support levels would be. one thing that you need to understand about this analysis is that the numbers on the sequence are simply the sum of two preceding terms. The sequence is also known to continue to infinity.

One remarkable feature of this sequence is the fact that each number is ~1.618 times greater than one that precedes it. That said, the Fibonacci retracement has been shown to suffer similar drawback as other universal trading tools. Therefore, it is critical that you use it in conjunction with other key indicators.

Back-testing

This is a general method used to see how well a strategy would have performed ex-post. The thing with back testing is that it assesses how viable a trading strategy is by simply uncovering how it is likely to play out with the use of historical data. In the event that back-testing works, this gives traders more confidence to apply it henceforth.

When optimizing your trading strategy, back testing would be the best way to go. When you simulate a trading strategy on the basis of historical data, you gain access to results that help you analyze risks and profitability before risking actual capital.

One thing you need to bear in mind is that if the back-test is conducted well and gives positive outcomes, then this is an assurance that your trading strategy is sound and has a chance of yielding profits when it is implemented. If the back-test is conducted well but the outcome is suboptimal, then there is a need to either alter or reject the strategy.

Key takeaways

- The market orders often get filled in an active market but not necessarily in the price the trader intended.
- Limit orders may or may not get filled and this depends on the manner in which the market is moving.
- Avoid setting take profit levels at random prices.
- Traders use mean reversion to find an edge and then build their trading strategies around it.
- Averaged data obscures important information on prices because the actual daily closing price is not seen on the Heikin-Ashi chart.
- When optimizing your trading strategy, back testing would be the best way to go.

Chapter 5: Guiding Principles And The Psychology Of A Successful Swing Trader

Simplicity Always Beats Complexity

One thing you should note about the investment industry is the fact that it is filled with complex terminologies and very busy charts. What is unfortunate is that most beginner traders confuse complexity as a requirement for one to succeed in the market.

Well, the truth is, you don't need any complexity in trading. There is no need for complex charts, data or even indicators for you to make a good trading decision of investment. It is often easy to get caught up in intellectual pursuits that we allow that to completely override our money-making efforts.

It is important that you stay simple when trading. Don't let being right or the desire to get great calls override the real reason why you are in the market. Being successful in trading does not mean complex screens, methods and tools, several technical indicators, or days staring at the screens.

What you need is the ability to adjust your opinion, have the fortitude to accept when you are wrong, get quality information, and have the ability to find confluences of support, resistance and unique thoughts about them.

How To Systematize Success: Plan – Do – Check – Act

When you are trading, one most important thing is to ensure that you have a trading plan.

Plan: what you need to do is plan a change and then test it. the main aim is to determine whether there is need for modification of the process for things to be more beneficial.

Do: the next thing is for you to implement that change and then try to test it on a small scale to ascertain the outcome.

Check: once you test the change, the results you obtain are relevant in determining what the important lessons are. Here, it is critical to note what went right, wrong and whether the changed worked out well or not. You can know how the change impacted the process by reviewing a 30,000-foot-level control chart and carrying out hypothesis tests.

Act: finally, it is important to note whether you would like to adopt the change, abandon it or redo the whole PDCA cycle. When you do not get any significant value from the process as you had initially anticipated, then it is safe to terminate the decision.

If the change is expected to create adherence issues or bring about minimal improvements, then it is safe to abort or repeat the cycle. In other words, you are repeating the process because the amount of improvement is not as much as you had anticipated. However, you might have already identified opportunities for change enhancement.

Once your main objective is met, then the final thing is for you to standardize the whole process. The power of this process lies in its simplicity and inductive use of logic. While it is also easy to understand, it can be challenging to attain on an ongoing basis mainly because of difficulty associated with analytical judgment of the hypothesis.

Plan: Setting your goals, targets and strategies

When you start trading, there are so many questions you need to ask. Truth is, with all the information out there, it can be challenging to decide where to begin. However, you should set goals, targets and strategize but chances are that most goals traders make are the wrong kind.

The goals that you set in the beginning will help determine whether you are going to make money or lose money. Therefore, it is important that you make your goals about the process and emulating all the traits professional traders portray.

The first one is by ensuring that you have a plan. In business school, we are taught to start any business with a business plan. If you didn't know, trading is a business! This means that each time you trade, you have to trade according to a well-thought-out, and calculated plan.

Your trading plan should tell you how to enter trades and exit trades. It should include ways you intend to manage money. In other words, the whole plan should be well-detailed with risk parameters to look out for, markets to be traded, position size, whether you intend to use filters as trade signals, the market environments to trade and how you intend to determine such things as trends and ranges among others.

In short, your goal should be to come up with a plan before you trade.

Do: Setting up your trading routine

When a certain dollar amount is your goal, you will ensure that you push to achieve that goal irrespective of opportunities being present or not. The truth is, the market does not present statistical probability of trading opportunities always. In fact, you will be better off sitting on your hands in most instances.

However, this does not really work well for most people. Most people are looking to continually do something. The thing is, in the market this can be slow and risks eroding your profits during good trading times.

Understand that trading when the times are slow or when you make impulsive trades that are out of scope requires your immediate attention. Therefore, one of your goals should be to be disciplined as much as possible so that you only trade as outlined on your plan.

Check and act

One thing that you need to note is that a complex strategy can be quite alluring. So many people think that just because something is complex it is highly likely to work. You need to avoid being fancy with your analysis and trading strategies. Don't make your winning plan complex.

What you need to do is check the plan you have that it is realistic and simple, and then act on it. If you fail to check and act, chances are that you will destroy the profitability of it. If you truly like the stock market, then ensure that you stick to trading stocks.

The bottom line here is for you to ensure that you are not constantly tinkering. This way, your performance will improve. Instead of always trying to switch the market, analysis method or the strategy, simply stick to your plan, check through it and action. However, if you feel the need to rework it occasionally, ensure that you keep all revisions simple so that you don't end up making things overly complex.

How to set up a trade journal

When trading, one of the most impactful and highly leveraged activities traders adopt is keeping track of their trades with the help of a trading journal. When you keep a trading journal, you ensure that you are keeping track of your experiences in the market so that you can come back to them later for lessons.

When you develop a trading journal/system, the most important thing is to save ideas in then and then test results. In other words, when you enter a certain position, you simply need to record everything about the trade. Ensure that you capture all your thoughts and contemplations when making a trade. This means that when you later have a "what was I thinking" moment in the future, all your answers will be found in the journal.

When setting up a trading journal, ensure that it has the following; trade date, number of shares and the reason you chose them, stock symbol, whether they are sold long/short, what triggered the entry signal and exit signal, where was your initial stop, did you move your stops and why, what was the reasons for your exit position?

Also, when you set up the trading journal, it is important that you keep track of not just your trades but beyond. For instance, the internet articles that influenced your thoughts, what the leading and lagging industries were and the charts that helped you through the process.

Even though keeping a journal is key, it is critical if you regularly review it. Therefore, set aside some time each week or month to just go through your trades to identify key mistakes and missed opportunities. Ensure that you are brutally honest with yourself by simply stepping back, taking a cold and hard look at the decisions you made when trading.

In short, your trading journal should be the soil that nurtures your growth.

Key takeaways

- There is no need for complex charts, data or even indicators for you to make a good trading decision.
- If the change is expected to create adherence issues or bring about minimal improvements, then it is safe to abort or repeat the cycle.
- Make your goals about the process and emulating all the traits professional traders portray.
- When you keep a trading journal, you ensure that you are keeping track of your experiences in the market so that you can come back to them later for lessons.

- Your trading journal should be the soil that nurtures your growth.

Chapter 6: How To Choose The Right Financial Instruments

Stocks

When you buy stocks, you become a small shareholder. If the company you buy the stocks is successful, then chances are that you will also benefit from the price gains and dividends. You also get a voting right at the shareholder table.

Some of the reasons why people buy stocks is for the sake of capital appreciation, dividend payment and influence the company. On the other hand, companies often issue stocks to pay off their debt, launch new products, expand into new markets, and enlarge facilities.

There are several types of stocks;

- Common stocks
- Preferred stocks
- Growth stocks
- Income stocks
- Value stocks
- Blue chip stocks

One of the benefits of investing in stocks is the fact that they offer a great opportunity for capital appreciation in the long term. Therefore, if you are willing to stay with the stocks for over 15 years, you are sure to get strong positive returns.

Note that stock prices often fluctuate up and down and there is no guarantee that the company you hold their stocks will grow and do very well in the market. This means that when you invest in stocks, you risk losing your money.

If the company you hold stocks for goes bankrupt and the assets are liquidated, it is the role of the common stockholders to take the last line in sharing the proceeds. The nod holders get paid first and whatever is left (or nothing) is shared among the common stockholders.

In spite the fact that companies may not be in danger of failing, chances are that their stocks will fluctuate up and down. Large companies often lose their money when they have to sell at stock prices below what they initially paid for. It is important to note that these market fluctuations can be unnerving to the investors. This is mainly because these prices are affected by factors inside the company such as faulty products; or events outside the company that are beyond the company's control such as politics.

So, how do you buy and sell stocks? There are so many ways you can buy and sell stocks. Some of these include direct stock plans, stock fund, dividend reinvestment plans, and discount or full-service broker.

For direct stock plans, there are companies that allow you to buy and sell stocks directly through a broker enabling you to save on commissions. However, you may have to pay other forms of fees to the plan such as transfer shares paid to the broker selling them.

One thing you need to note about direct stock plans is that they will not permit you to trade at a specific market price and time. Rather, the company prefers to trade shares for the plan at a time they have set e.g. daily, weekly, or monthly. Also, depending on the kind of plan you have, you may choose to automate your buys so that the cost is significantly reduced from your savings account automatically.

Dividend reinvestment plans permits one to buy as much shares of stocks as possible by simply reinvesting dividend payments into the company. This means that you have to sign an agreement with the company to have things done. It is therefore important that you check with your brokerage company for any additional charges you might have to incur.

Discounts (full-service broker) often involve brokers trading shares for customers at commission. The other way to buy is stock funds. This is a kind of mutual fund that invests primarily in stocks and depending on the policy or investment objective, the stock fund may be focused on a certain stock.

Options

These simply refer to contracts by which a seller offers the buyer the right and not the obligation to trade a specific number of units of assets at a predetermined price within a set duration. Here, the buyer has an option of either calling or putting the underlying assets. There are a number of factors that determine the price of an option. These include the difference between the current price and the strike price.

When you decide to purchase a call option, you are entitled to buy its underlying value too. This is something that only stands for a specified duration and price. The most important thing to note here is that for this right, you are supposed to pay a premium expressed in the price of stocks on the option contract. The underlying value of the option contract is composed of about 100 shares.

Buying a call option means that you speculate on the increase in its underlying value. The higher the value, the higher your option increases in value. The higher the underlying value, the higher the value of the option contract.

It is important to note that with an option contract, termination happens upon expiry, which is indicated on the contract. If it is a monthly option, expiration happens on the third Friday of every month. For instance, if you purchase one contract C RD JAN 2020 9, you are entitled to 100 shares RD to the third Friday of January 2019 for only 9 euros/share.

However, when you choose to buy a put option, it is the exact opposite of the call option. Here, you entitled to sell its underlying value during a certain duration, with the hope that the underlying value will decrease. This means that your profits will depend on selling the value of your options to another person at a higher price compared to the price of the stock. Truth is, if you buy a call option or a put option, you will not lose more than your call.

Exchange-Traded Funds (ETF)

The ETF passive funds and trackers are basically one and the same product. ETFs simply refer to simple investment where you buy a portion of an index like DAX, AEX, and FTSE among others. This kind of investment is referred to as index investment.

In case an FTSE increases, your purchase ETF grow in value, and the vice versa is also true. One thing you will note about ETFs is that they are transparent and offer a good spread and a low cost of management. Because of its simplicity, they are growing in popularity today.

One thing that makes these ETFs successful is the fact that they are a cheaper alternative to other investment funds, particularly a low cost of management. Interestingly, there are a number of ETFs that already follow the 0.15% index value making them even more attractive.

When you compare this to an investment set at 1.5%, you actually get to save about 1% on yearly cost. Additionally, the outcome of ETFs on average are way better compared to investment funds, actively managed by fund managers whose main aim is to perform above the benchmark index.

However, a majority of mutual funds stay below the index they aim at exceeding. This means that with an ETF, you not only pay a lower cost of management but also increase your likelihood of getting higher returns on your investment fund with the same benchmark.

So, why should you invest in ETFs? Well, this is a question that so many people ask. Just like investment funds, ETFs are a great investment tool for a beginner. This is mainly because they allow you to work at a lower threshold that enables you to boost your asset growth. Additionally, they are quite transparent and offer an attractive spread. They also offer you the opportunity to invest in themes and sectors that would otherwise be inaccessible.

Cryptocurrencies

This simply refers to digital currencies using a decentralized network control compared to conventional currencies typically managed by the bank. The world's first cryptocurrency is referred to as the Bitcoin, and has seen a dramatic increase in its popularity, adoption, and volatility.

Some of Bitcoin's main competitors include Litecoin, Ethereum, Ripple, and Bitcoin cash. The pricing of various cryptocurrencies is often derived from their value and exchanges often dominated by the US dollar.

Trading cryptocurrency can be quite daunting for any beginner but the good thing is that such books as this are there to offer you guidance. One thing you need to note is that you have to familiarize yourself with a number of things and you will be set. The very first thing you need to do is understand what cryptocurrencies are and what they are all about.

What you need to note is that one cryptocurrency is different from the other, hence the need to understand each as more than just any other digital number that people use as an alternative to physical money. When you make transactions using cryptocurrency, you are sure that the process is error proof, hence making it a great option for investors.

The second thing that you need to do is select a broker who will help you understand all basics involved when trading cryptocurrency. Once you identify a reliable broker, the next thing is for you to sign up. The good thing is that most online brokers offer investors an opportunity to create dummy accounts for them to perfect their trading skills first. The other good thing about these platforms is that they have more features other than cryptocurrencies alone that you may be interested in trying out.

Considering the fact that there are thousands of brokers out there that claim that their services are perfect of investors, it is critical that you have an idea of what brokers are reliable and trustworthy as far as trading cryptocurrencies is concerned.

If you visit Binaly.com, you will get access to information about binary options and the best ranking brokers based on investor reviews. This way, you can make informed choices based on this important information.

There are so many reasons why you should invest in cryptocurrencies aside from the fact that they are increasingly growing. Some of these reasons include;

Fraud

There is a lot of risk associated with giving your credit card information to merchants. Some of these risks are identity theft that hackers can use to pull a similar amount of trade from your credit account. On the other hand, cryptocurrencies allow you to use pushing to send a certain amount to the broker without necessarily sending along your personal information.

Universal access

Most people today access the internet using varied kinds of devices. Most of the internet users have not been on the traditional system of exchange, making the crypto market greatly advantageous. All you need here is a bitcoin wallet which you easily install from App store or Google Play.

Immediate settlements

When buying property, you often need a middleman, which is accompanied by additional delays, fees, and even unanticipated difficulties. However, when you use cryptocurrencies, there is no middlemen involved opening an opportunity for future settlements.

Affordable fees

Most crypto-transactions are not accompanied with transaction fees. This is mainly because the network often compensates miners. However, there are third party services like Coinbase that operate like PayPal meaning that they charge a fee but the fee is not exorbitant.

You are the owner

This is one of the most important advantages of trading cryptocurrencies. The only thing you need is a wallet and the account is yours and should not be accessed by anyone else.

Let us consider the case of PayPal where they have the power to freeze your accounts without even letting you know. With cryptocurrency, you are given a private key that is your alone. Additionally, trading crypto is easy to learn and permits you to use more than a single currency at the same time.

Unlike the stock market where you are needed to meet a number of conditions, trading cryptocurrencies has no conditions and you can start right away as long as you have internet access.

Key takeaways

- Investing in stocks is the fact that they offer a great opportunity for capital appreciation in the long term.

- If the company you hold stocks for goes bankrupt and the assets are liquidated, it is the role of the common stockholders to take the last line in sharing the proceeds.

- When you decide to purchase a call option, you are entitled to buy its underlying value too.

- Select a broker who will help you understand all basics involved when trading cryptocurrency.

Conclusion

There you have it. Congratulations for reading all through the book. Indeed, if the market always seems to move lower after you buy things are going to begin to change in your favor. If you always wish that your trades end sooner because you hate watching your P&L fluctuate, then now you have all the tools to make things better for you.

Swing trading will help you identify intermediate-term opportunities use a wide range of technical analysis tools. Therefore, if you have not established an intimate relationship with technical analysis, now is the time to practice what you have learnt in this book.

One thing you need to note is that for every trade, you need to assess the risk/reward ratio. Your main aim here is to profit from a price move you anticipated from the very beginning of the trade. It is through swing trading that you will gain exposure to overnight risks, where prices have a likelihood of gapping and opening the next sessions at substantial price difference.

Each time you trade, ensure that you use already established risk/return ratio considering the profit targets and stop loss orders.

So, what are you still waiting for?

Find a suitable brokerage firm, sign up and start trading today.

Your best days are still up ahead of you. You better catch up!

If this book helped you to gain insight into how to swing trade successfully, kindly leave us a review/comments.

Recommended Trading Resources
To Start With

- Trading simulators:
  - Investopedia: https://www.investopedia.com/simulator/?source=dfpros-sim&subid=dfp-ros-sim
- Broker:
  - Ally.com: https://www.ally.com/invest/?tk=1
- Stock screener:
  - Chartmill.com: https://www.chartmill.com/ o Finviz.com: https://finviz.com/
- Graphing utility:
  - TradingView.com
- Back-testing:
  - PastStat.com
  - StockBackTest.com
  - MarketInOut.com

Printed in the USA
CPSIA information can be obtained
at www.ICGtesting.com
CBHW071614300924
15156CB00037B/942